A MATTER OF FIFTY HOUSES

BOOKS BY *WALTER HARD*

SOME VERMONTERS
1928—*Gorham Press. Out of print.*

SALT OF VERMONT
1931—*Stephen Daye Press. Out of print.*

MOUNTAIN TOWNSHIP
1933—*Harcourt, Brace and Company. Out of print.*
1946 and 1963—Stephen Daye Press. Revised and enlarged editions.

VERMONT VINTAGE
1937—*Stephen Daye Press. Out of print.*

VERMONT VALLEY
1937—*Harcourt, Brace and Company. Out of print.*
1959—Vermont Books, new edition.

VERMONT SALT AND VINTAGE
Combining SALT OF VERMONT *and* VERMONT VINTAGE
1946 and 1955—Stephen Daye Press. Revised and enlarged editions.
Published also in 1941 as WALTER HARD'S VERMONT

THE CONNECTICUT
1947—*Holt, Rinehart & Winston, Rivers of America Series.*

A MATTER OF FIFTY HOUSES
1952—*Vermont Books*

VERMONT NEIGHBORS
1960—*Vermont Books*

VERMONT SAMPLER
A "sampling" from the three Vermont Books editions.
1963—Vermont Books, paperbound.
A collector's edition, specially printed and clothbound,
numbered and signed, was limited to five hundred copies, and is out of print.

With MARGARET HARD
THIS IS VERMONT
1936—*Stephen Daye Press. Out of print.*

Walter Hard is poet, annalist, anecdote finder. I find his Yankees more fascinating than most of the Greeks in Greek mythology. He and I are of the same school in believing that an anecdote of sufficient pith and portent is in essence a true poem. I treasure and reread his volumes.

—CARL SANDBURG

There it lies
Dozing peacefully under the maples;
A church, a school, a tavern, some stores,
And a matter of fifty houses. . .
A sleepy village in a peaceful valley,
Yet, friend, there life stages its drama. . .
Fifty houses offering the life of the race.

—WALTER HARD
THE VILLAGE

A MATTER OF
FIFTY HOUSES

by WALTER HARD

VERMONT BOOKS
MIDDLEBURY, VERMONT

10/1983

©

FOURTH PRINTING

Cover Drawing By
RUTH MOORE WILLIAMS

FOR MY CHILDREN'S CHILDREN

Whose roots
go seven generations deep
in Vermont

FOREWORD

LANDSCAPE has its way with the people who live within it. Give it a little time and it becomes a major factor in human life as surely as its twin younger brothers, death and taxes. Dwell among the Vermont hills and valleys for a decade and, while you are still regarded as a foreigner by your neighbors, your friends of another day and place will already observe the beginnings of an inevitable victory. Ancestral Latin blood may sing in your veins, or you may inherit a loquacious sentimentality from prototypes of Goethe's young Werther, but Vermont *vincit omnia*.

The wedding of a land and its people is not necessarily to be considered, like a wedding in popular fiction, a happy ending. But it is a beginning which may result, as many of the best marriages do, in a composite personality. Just as in some instances it seems impossible to think of a husband without thinking of his wife, or of a wife without her husband, it has now become difficult indeed to disassociate Vermont from Vermonters. The country and the people are together an identity.

The books of Walter Hard are penetrating and poetic studies of that identity. Let no one be innocent enough to think of them as groupings of guileless and separate anecdotes. They are bound into an inseparable and continuous and artistic whole by the cement of the author's philosophy. They present a likeness of a land and its people that deserves a place in the gallery of the best that has been done by the regionalists of the earth. And like that best, wherever it has been achieved, these creations transcend the limits of region. In them physical boundaries recede and a corner of the universe becomes universal.

A MATTER OF FIFTY HOUSES is, I believe, the most mature and meaningful of all of Walter Hard's volumes. It is a summation of American rural life that every sensitive and serious student of Americana will read with delight. It is wisely and at times bitterly humorous, poignantly human, deeply poetic. Its readers will discover, before they have read many pages, that A MATTER OF FIFTY HOUSES is a matter of a world.

CARL CARMER

Irvington-on-Hudson,
June, 1952.

CONTENTS

A MATTER OF FIFTY HOUSES

Timepiece

Waiting for the crowd to gather,
The auctioneer was putting a table before the front door.
An old man leaned against a tree and watched.
He said the Doctor had died ten years before.
They'd just got around to settle the estate.
"How old? He'd 'a been eighty-two if he'd lived to now.
That ain't old; I'm eighty-seven."
He tried to square his bent shoulders.
"Oldest man in the village now" he added.
The blacksmith's chimney, on a corner of the Village Green,
Poured forth a cloud of black smoke.
On the other side there was a red brick church
And back of it the weather-beaten stones of the burying ground.
There the Doctor rested undisturbed by midnight calls.
"Take out those telephone poles and those automobiles,
It'd look just as it did the day the Doctor set up here.
I started drivin' for him a few months later."
He stopped to listen to the auctioneer for a minute.
"Drove 'til he died; had t' keep horses
For winter and mud time even after he got him a car."
The auctioneer was getting bids on the Doctor's big chair
And his desk, strangely free of bottles and papers.
After a while a clock was put out on the table.
It had gilded pillars on the corners
And wood sides made to look like marble.
At once the old man was alert.
He bid a quarter.
He followed the rising bids, a quarter at a time,
Until they got up to two thirty.
The old mans voice was shaking when he made it forty.
He tried to look unconcerned when the auctioneer asked for more.
"First and last time. Are you all done?"
The old man begged with his eyes as he looked around.
"Who'll make it fifty? Forty I'm offered.
All done?"
It seemed minutes to the old man before he said:
"Sold to that man over by that tree."
The old man pushed through the crowd.

3

He came back and set the clock on the marble carriage block.
He opened the back and let the hammer fall.
"I've set and heered that strike many a night
Waitin' fer the Doctor t' get his things ready,
Whilst the wind was slappin' th' snow against th' winder."
He shut the back and ran his hand over the smooth top.
"Yes, this old clock ticked the Doctor out
And now I reckon mebbe it'll tick me out too."
He put it under his arm and started across the Green,
The gong sounding as he stepped.

A Robbery

The usual silence of the village street
Was punctuated by the staccato explosions
Of a gasoline engine sawing wood back of the store.
The steady putt would change to a slower tempo
As the saw took hold of a piece of body maple.
Sometimes, on a big stick, it would seem about to give up.
Just as it seemed sure to stop it would cut through
And away would go the freed engine in joyous abandon.
Finally the last stick was cut
And the engine was quiet, steaming in the cold air.
The crew of three pulled off their bulky mittens
And walked around to the front of the store.
They stamped the snow from their moccasins on the porch.
Inside they held their hands toward the ruddy stove.
Mel Wlison took his cap off and turned the ear flaps in.
Tom Stone was in his usual chair reading the SIFTER.
He came from 'Derry and always took the home town paper.
"Well, Thomas, what's the news from over the hill?"
Mel Wilson unbuttoned his coat and sat down on the bench.
Tom finished reading a piece and then looked at Mel.
"Say" he said "you used t' know Hen Bradford didn't ye?"
Mel admitted he was well acquainted with Hen.
"Wal, by thunder" Tom went on as he looked at the paper again,
"There's a piece here about how a feller workin' fer him,
Stole his horse and runned off with his woman."

4

Mel leaned forward all interest.
"No—you don't say—stole his horse and—
By judast, not that chestnut pacer
You don't 'spose?"

A Short Month

One reason people employed Ellery
Was that he always agreed to undertake anything
That was suggested to him.
No matter how much it might involve,
He made the accomplishment seem short and simple.
Of course the village people knew Ellery.
They might hire him for short jobs
Of painting or papering or puttering.
If he didn't show up when he said he would
They'd hitch up and drive down the valley after him.
People who bought places and wanted them fixed for summer
Usually landed on Ellery's doorstep.
He'd spend an afternoon going over a job
And in the end he'd have given the impression
That he'd hercules the job through in short order.
Of course he got the job right then and there.
Then his new employer would go back to the city
And tell the men in the office about Ellery.
No bother up there in God's country about unions
And no high paid specialists for each little thing.
Just Ellery.
By the next autumn he'd find Ellery still making promises
To come and finish what he'd started and left.
Usually others had to be found to finish the job.
All through July and August he'd promise to come "next week."
He always had an excuse ready when he got cornered
But he usually kept out of his employer's way if possible.
One exasperated householder who had spent his vacation
Waiting around for Ellery to come and help him
Met him face to face in front of the store.
Ellery took his heated accusations in silence.

"You agreed week after week to come all through August.
You never came. Why?"
Ellery shifted his hat and spoke reassuringly.
"Well, I'll tell you, Mr. Newcomer,
August didn't turn out t' be as long as I callated."

Deeds, Good and Bad

In the index of the book for recording deeds
In the office of the Town Clerk
Abner Hollins' transactions filled considerable space.
He bought woodland and farms and meadow land.
Then he'd cut it up or join it together and sell
Perhaps a part to one person and some to another.
He was generally considered a sharp trader
And usually, when he'd enlarged the area of his holdings
By including a few feet from a neighbor
There might be some heated words but no action.
On mountain woodlots surveys were not frequent and not very sure.
His family had moved so often
That his wife got so she didn't tack the carpets down.
One time Abner did get into real trouble.
He sold a piece of woodland that had considerable ash on it.
There was a demand for ash just then
And the buyer sold off considerable on the stump.
When cutting began, the owner next got a court order.
This was served on Abner's customers and they came back at Abner.
He'd sold quite a number of acres more than he owned.
The young lawyer Abner hired settled out of court
But he told Abner he just couldn't see
How he could keep track of where his lines were.
"You sell off a few acres here and there and then the remainder.
Three or four transactions. How can you keep 'em straight?"
"Wal" Abner admitted, "I ain't allas certain.
But if I get me a good cash offer I sell.
Then I wait t' see what happens."

Mrs. Fisher's Bait

When tourists began to stop in the village
Some of the people were glad to see them
And enjoyed giving directions about the roads.
Mrs. Fisher, who lived in the cottage next to the store,
Always liked to meet anything that was new to her.
Any stranger who looked at her for more than a minute
Was sure to get a welcoming smile
And, unless he hurried away, an earful of conversation.
There was never any malice in her gossip
But when she heard something of interest
She liked to share it.
She generally sat on her porch in a small rocker
And many people stopped to pass the time of day.
One summer, after the tourists had begun to come in force,
Mrs. Humble, a stranger-hater who lived across from Mrs. Fisher,
Noticed that Mrs. Fisher had dragged out onto her porch
An old Boston rocker which had been her father's.
From time to time a stranger would be strolling past
And she noticed they often stopped and looked at the rocker.
Not infrequently they'd go up on the porch and sit in it
While Mrs. Fisher, in her small rocker, visited with them.
Mrs. Humble got madder and madder at her neighbor.
In the first place she couldn't stand her visiting with strangers.
Then, knowing how little Mrs. Fisher had,
She thought she was crazy not to sell the old chair.
Finally she had to go across and free her mind.
"You must have no end o' chances t' get a good price fer that chair.
You got more chairs now that you'll ever set on."
Mrs. Fisher rocked in her small rocker.
"Why Mis' Humble, I wouldn't think o' sellin' that chair.
From the first day I set it out here
I've met more int'restin' folks stoppin' t' ask about it,
Than I'd gen'rally git t' know in a lifetime."
She rocked a minute, looking at the old Boston rocker.
"Yes, it makes out t' be the best introducer I ever did see."

Needing a Change

The Grover farm lay on the top of the ridge
Which separated the two valleys.
The road to it, steep and winding,
Was always known as the "Hill Road."
Whoever had cleared the land on the hill top
Had found rich soil waiting,
Made by the trees he'd cut to clear it.
The long lines of stone walls
Which marked the boundaries
Were monuments to the unending toil
Of the men who had harvested the never-ending crop of stones.
Elijah Grover was the third generation on the place.
He'd taken over in his early twenties.
He was tall and rawboned and a glutton for work.
He never kept a hired man for long
For he expected him to do as much as he himself did.
He was standing by the iron kettle
Which was half inside the barnyard and half out.
Ice cold water from a sure spring poured into it.
Elijah was talking to a man in a car.
"Yes sir" he was saying,
"I'm seventy-eight, or I will be next month if I live."
The visitor thought he seemed rugged enough
So he should easily make his birthday at least.
"Well I've had the bitter with th' sweet.
Seventy-eight year of it's quite a spell.
Ain't been feeling too good this winter."
He put his foot on the water kettle.
"Sometimes I wonder if it agrees with me here" he added.

An Abandoned Road

That hill road had been a proud road.
It had gone straight up to get away from the village quickly.
It hadn't made any devious easy turnings
To get to the higher ground.

8

It stopped just once so that you could look back at what you'd done
And get your breath to finish what you'd started.
Having got the hard part over all at once
It took its way more leisurely along the ridge.
Almost level, as Vermont roads go,
It kept to the foothills
Which brace the mountains against the sky.
Then it was a cross-state road.
On it rocking stagecoaches used to go
With an extra team to get them past that first hard grade.

Now its days are over.
The village grew up in the valley
And the road followed the winding stream.
Grass grew between the ruts of the hill road.
A few old settlers, who'd worked the road when they were young,
Made them keep it open.
Then their sons made roads straight down from their farms
Sooner to meet the valley road that went to towns.

Now, still a proud road, it climbs the hill
With enough houses near the village to keep it.
Beyond the last house it fades into the woods.
Bush-grown cellar holes and dying apple trees
Pay no taxes to keep up a road.
You can follow it on foot perhaps
But at times you'll have to look toward the sky
To be sure you're on it.
Even the stone walls which marked the farms
Have been taken by the encroaching forest.
Here and there you'll find signs of a clearing
Where a few gray-barked patriarchal maples
Remember where the farmhouse stood.
If you look carefully you may find the two tracks
Where the iron-shod wheels packed the rocks and soil
Too hard even for seedlings to find a root-hold.
It takes years on years of rotting leaves
To wipe out a proud hill road.

Guide For Guests

Amos lived alone near the top of the mountain.
He did a little trapping
And each year's town report showed
He'd received wages for work on the road.
Of course he had a good garden and a woodlot
And take it all in all he managed very well.
The fall after the big flood
He worked more than usual on the road.
Then he worked down the valley on a WPA job
But the long cold ride in the pickup truck they sent
Was too uncomfortable and he quit.
He was sitting by the kitchen table.
The teakettle was singing on the stove
While outside the snow was falling in big flakes.
On the table Amos had a bottle of ink and some paper.
He was composing a letter.
His labor-knotted hands were not used to holding
Such a delicate tool as a pen
And his spelling vocabulary was limited.
When a neighbor dropped in he was glad of an excuse
To rest from his epistolary labors.
He felt he must explain the unusual task
He had been caught at.
"I got me money saved up t' go vis'tin' " he said.
"Callate t' go to my cousin's to Boston.
Got me enough saved up t' get me there and some fer presents.
Writin' her I'm acomin'."
"If you only got enough t' git there
How 'are you figurin' t' git back home?"
Amos reached for a stick of wood.
"That's their hunt" he said.

Aunt Delia

Aunt Delia was as much a part of her garden
As the flowers that grew in it.
Her understanding of human nature

10

And her patience with its peculiarities
Seemed to have their roots in the rich garden soil.
From it she drew something vital
Just as her flowers did.
When people came back after years of absence
They always made first for Aunt Delia's,
Knowing they'd have a hearty welcome and a listening ear.
She lived alone and kept her house in order
But from May to late October her garden was her dwelling place.
On pleasant days passers-by on the street
Could see her faded sunbonnet bobbing up and down
As she attended her growing charges.
When she was ninety she had the first illness
She could remember that made her take to her bed.
She didn't seem to gain much strength
And her friends thought she might never be up again.
By the time the first seed catalog arrived in February
Aunt Delia showed considerable interest in it.
The doctor remarked a few weeks later that he believed
That new tonic he'd left for her was doing her good.
She was a little late in getting out to her garden
But that summer her flowers seemed to flourish more than ever.
Someone asked her how she really was.
"Well, I have to rest quite often" she said
"But I seem to be left with this miserable cough.
I'd hate to go through life with that tagging along."

Respect for Old Age

Old Toddy had a reputation as a hunting dog
That extended far beyond the village.
He belonged to Bert Olney and was known
As "Bert Olney's Tod."
When he was about six Tod was the most important thing
In Bert's life, especially in hunting season.
When the snow was too deep even for hunting
Bert, with Tod at his feet, spent much of his time
With the other sitters around Brayley's store stove.
They'd all hear over and over the wonderful stories

Bert told of Tod's genius for hunting.
Every time his name was mentioned
Tod's tail would bang on the floor.
In winter, Tod had so much friendliness to express
That often his tail was bleeding on the tip,
From being whacked so hard and often on the floor.
When the bird season was on, the evening sessions at Brayley's
Were mostly taken up with stories of the day's experiences.
Bert always waited until last with his climax-capping yarn.
Then Tod began to show his age.
His legs got stiffer and stiffer.
In summer he spent most of his time sleeping in the sun.
Sometimes he'd move into the shade for a little while
But he seemed to like the warmth.
He'd get to his feet with a struggle
And follow Bert to the store where he'd flop down again and sleep.
That fall Bert took Tod out as usual.
He didn't go far from the village
And usually several shots would be heard from that direction.
When Bert didn't bring in any birds or any stories of them
People began to wonder what all the shooting was about.
Finally Ed Stone came on Bert and old Tod
Just after he'd shot twice.
Tod stood there pointing at a clump of bushes.
Bert seemed a little taken back.
Then he said "The old dog's nose ain't a bit o' good
And the old cuss can't see beyond the end of his nose.
When he points I just shoot m' gun off
Knowin' all th' time there ain't no birds there."
Tod stood there trembling, still pointing at the brush.
Bert stooped over and rubbed his ear.
"Don't want the old feller t' get the idee
I think he's a liar."

Short Rations for Mice and Men

In the school district where Steve Piper had taught
He had boarded around as had been the custom.
While this gave Steve a chance to know the families
And thus helped him to understand his pupils
He found the constant changing was not comfortable.
So when he had a chance to move to a school up north
Where they paid a weekly salary and let the teacher
Pay for his own board where he chose,
Steve decided to make the change
Especially since the weekly stipend was so much higher.
When he got to his new stand
The only place he could find to board
Was in the family of one of the school directors.
It was neat and clean at the Albers'
And Steve settled down with a sigh of relief.
It wasn't long before Steve found out
That the Albers were not used to hearty meals.
Steve himself was not equipped with a very demanding appetite
So he didn't notice the lacks so much.
The other boarder worked in Mr. Alber's store
And he liked three square meals a day.
As soon as he got to know Steve well enough
He poured out his complaints of Mrs. Alber's stinginess.
Steve noticed that she complained about giving to Grange suppers
And that the day after, their fare was more skimpy than ever.
One night, after a very sketchy supper,
When it came time to go upstairs
The store clerk stopped to complain by Steve's door.
As he turned to go into his own room
Mrs. Alber, who had been fixing the griddle cake batter,
Called from the foot of the stairs to her husband:
"Eben" she shouted, all excitement, "There's a mouse in th' butt'ry.
What 'll I do?"
The bed creaked in the Albers' room.
Before Mr. Alber was awake enough to know what was going on,
The clerk, with a sudden access of courage, shouted:
"Lock th' damned mouse in the butt'ry
And let him starve t' death."

13

Weedy Widows

The Thorne sisters were generally known as "The Widows."
Sometimes they were referred to as "Them Weepin' Willows."
Their widowhood was their one claim to distinction.
Etta's husband had been the town's lawyer.
When he died his widow donned black and a widow's veil
And was rarely seen out except on the day
She was able to take her floral tribute to the burying ground.
After two years her sister's husband's remains
Were placed in a plot near Etta's.
The sister moved in with Etta, clothed in the same garments.
The two were seldom seen except at church
And on their way to and from the cemetery.
It had been generally understood
That neither marriage had been a happy one
And the village failed to understand
The lavish display of sorrow.
They grew old together in the shade-drawn house.
They always appeared on the street together
And they always wore their thick black veils,
Which brought out the shut-in pallor of their faces.
One spring day Henry Landon was strolling home
Enjoying the feel of the clean warm air.
As he drew near to the burying ground
He met Eber Howe and they stopped to visit.
All of a sudden Henry grabbed Eber by the arm.
Out from the deep shade of the evergreens at the cemetery entrance
The two widows were moving slowly with heads bent.
They seemed like ominous black shadows.
"Eber, good God! Look at that.
You don't suppose they're all comin' out do you?"

A Head Injury

Nate's seasons on the farm
Were always from a week to a month later
Than those recognized by other farmers in the valley.
Late with his plowing, as now, his planting would be late.

He put off cultivating until usually it was hard
To follow the thin line of crop
Through the jungle of weeds.
The harvesting of what there was to harvest
Was late because of the late maturing, of course.
Added to this accumulation of lateness was the special delay
Which came from putting off the harvesting chore.
It not infrequently happened that there was no harvesting.
Winter snows often covered lines of dismal cornstalks.
Nate was this day plowing a piece that lay along the road.
He had stopped to look down the valley
Which bent to the west below his farm a half mile.
Nate might be weak on cultivating the soil
But he was strong on cultivating many things
Which loomed large among the durable satisfactions.
Looking at the mountains always gave him something.
An automobile interrupted his resting
By stopping across the road.
A man approached with a map in hand.
"What's the matter with the old fellow
Who lives a couple of houses below?
I asked him about directions but he acted funny
And wandered all over the lots in his talk."
Nate stroked his beard and smiled a little.
"Well, they say he got kicked in the head by a horse.
That was some time ago. I guess if anything ran out
It all did."

Contrast at the County Seat

The road drops quickly to the village.
There the Green spreads out on either side.
On the left stands the County House
Offering hospitality to the traveler,
While on the end of the hostelry
Are the barred windows of the county jail.
The County House is old and sedate in spite of the row
Of gayly painted chairs on its long porch.
There is the store still showing the simple lines

Of its ancient architecture in spite of the shining windows
Which reflect the row of red gas pumps
Where the hitching posts used to stand.
On the right the rambling tavern
Remains true to its pristine dignity,
Spotless in its white paint.
Beyond there is the house built for worship.
Between it and the tavern stands the court house,
Whose tall fluted pillars cast shadows on its white front—
A classic monument to the ancient dignity of the Law.
On the hills, plows are turning long straight furrows
And harrows are making fields smooth for planting.
Along the street women bend over flower beds
Behind white picket fences.
Joyful children race around the school yard,
Free for a moment from life's drudgeries.
The south wind stirs the new green leaves on the maples.

· · · · · · · ·

Inside the classic court house
A man is on trial for his life,
Accused of murdering a Chinaman.

Stiffness

Matilda Spinney had an excellent reputation as an educator.
Her select school for select young ladies
Had come to be the proper training ground
For those who belonged to a certain social stratum.
She gave the kind of training the mothers had had
And the mothers were evidently satisfied
With what such a system turned out.
There were a few concessions to modern trends
But in general it was held that what had been good
For the mothers was good for the daughters.
When Miss Spinney bought a summer place in the country
She organized it as she did her faculty,
And expected things done as the faculty carried out the curriculum.
The various men who tried to work for her

Found they must leave their own ideas outside the gate
Or stay outside themselves.
When she decided to take up horseback riding
She prepared to master the art by main force.
After an hour with a groom, she knew
All that she needed to be taught.
The next day over the protests of the riding master
She set forth on her own.
After three hours had passed, the riding master
Was preparing to send out a searching party
When Miss Spinney rode into the yard.
Her face was scarlet, her hair was tumbling down,
And the horse's mouth was hanging open.
As the groom lent a hand she started to dismount.
In spite of a set jaw she found she was too stiff to make it.
A second groom came out to help.
Miss Spinney finally ordered one to take her right "limb"
And the other her left.
As they raised her aloft, the riding master
Led the horse out from under.
The next day the Doctor, an old friend,
Said as he was leaving her room
"You'll get over the leg stiffness in a few days.
But by George, Matilda, it's too late
To do anything about that stiff neck of yours."

No Margin for Error

When Young Jim began to work in the bank
Some of the older men in the village
Were not quite sure he was fitted for the job.
Of course his father was still there all the time
But he was getting along in years.
Not that they had anything against Young Jim
But he hadn't steadied down.
He liked to go out to dances
And some said he played cards considerable too.
Then he played in the band.
That didn't seem quite suited to the dignity

They expected to find in their banker.
They couldn't do much about it
Because Old Jim practically owned the bank.
Gradually Young Jim made himself solid
With most of the uncertain elders
By his pleasant manner and willingness to listen.
So it came about that often Old Jim
Wouldn't go to the bank for several days
Leaving his son to run things alone.
One morning just after Young Jim had pulled up the shades
Eber Stevens came in and asked for some change.
He put down a twenty dollar bill.
"Goin' out t' peddle a beef I jest killed.
Don't figger on havin' t' trust nobody
'Cause I can't make change either."
Jim counted out the silver in piles
And shoved them under the grating.
"Guess that'll fix you up" he said,
As he went back to his book work.
After some time he looked up and saw Eber
Still standing there counting and restacking.
He put his pen back of his ear and got down from the stool.
"Didn't I give you enough?" he asked.
Eber's lips went on counting the last pile.
He stopped and looked at the money.
"I say, didn't I give you enough?" Jim repeated.
Eber sighed. "Jest barely" he said.

Alone

She was sitting on the kitchen porch.
From the south meadow the breeze
Brought the familiar summer sound of the mowing machine.
There wasn't any need to hurry with the peas she was shelling.
He wasn't riding that mowing machine.
He wouldn't be coming up to the watering trough with the team.
He wouldn't be washing his hot face with the cold water at the sink.
It had all happened so quickly
And her even-going mind caught up with changes slowly.

18

He'd never been sick before.
Any idea that his strong body might break
Had never come to make her ready for tragedy.
Others had come in to take charge.
As she looked back she felt as though
She had only come to the surface now and then.
Gradually she was piecing the whole thing together;
Filling in the gaps to make the days whole.
After the funeral there had been the family matters
Most of which had been settled by his relations.
Almost before she knew it there had been the auction
And the crowds of buyers and cruious ones.
She saw the herd he'd nurtured sold off in two hours.
She saw strangers dragging his hard-won farm machines away.
And now a neighbor was cutting the hay in the south meadow.
She was sitting alone on the kitchen porch
With no one to wait for.
The neighbors had been very kind
But she wasn't used to sharing with anyone but him—
Joy or sorrow.
She appreciated what people tried to say
But she couldn't think of anything to say back.
That very morning the young minister had been up.
He'd brought some flowers from his wife.
"You miss your husband very much" he had said.
"Yes" she said, rocking slowly,
"I've washed his shirts for over forty years."

Not To Be Despised

Peter Huggin's farm seemed to bear chiefly stones.
Evidently a retreating glacier had sat down to rest there
Ridding itself of some of its accumulated burden.
No matter how often Peter reloaded his stoneboat
Every time he plowed a new crop showed up.
In spite of the inhospitable look of the soil
Peter managed to raise good crops.
The story of his struggle was told
In the long lines of sturdy stone wall.

Perhaps it was this struggle with hardness
That had affected Peter's disposition.
He had become a stooped taciturn man,
Elderly in mind and body at fifty.
He refused to use any labor-saving devices,
Sticking to the methods and tools of his father.
One day he was harrowing a piece
That ran along the highway which led to the village.
A buggy came along the road and stopped
Waiting for Peter to draw near.
Peter stopped his team grudgingly,
And nodded toward the occupant of the buggy.
"What on earth do you expect will grow
On an acre of rocks like that?"
Disgusted, Peter prepared to leave.
Clucking to his team he said as they started,
"I'd have you know, stranger,
That buckwheat ain't any damned fool."

The Female Invasion

Ike Stubbs and Alfred Higgins
Were sitting on the porch of Brayley's store.
A bevy of women and girls had just come out
And climbed into the truck that had brought them from the lake.
Brayley came out lighting a stogie.
He wiped his brow and bald head with a blue handkerchief.
Ike and Alfred were gazing with fishy eyes
At the variously clad and unclad females
Who, with much laughter, were getting settled in the truck.
As they started off Ike removed his straw hat to air his head
While he aired his views.
"It's got so us men ain't got much left
The women havin' gen'rally taken everythin' over."
He leaned back and clasped his knee with his hairy hands.
"They wear our clothes, overhalls and all.
They smoke and they drink and mebbe chew; I heered so.
And when it comes t' just social cussin'
They can drag more into an ord'nary conversation

Than a man 'd need plowing a piece o' stony hillside."
Alfred Higgins rapped his pipe on his heel.
"That ain't th' worst of it, by judast" he said.
"They're takin' th' bread and butter right out a man's mouth.
They're runnin' machines in fact'ries. I seen pictures of 'em.
And I'm damned if one of the city girls
That's come into th' country t' do farm work
Wa'n't out runnin' a tractor at Judson's as I come by just now."
"Hadn't ought t' ever let 'em have th' vote" Brayley put in.
"Why they's a female woman runnin' one of New York's biggest stores.
Read about it in the paper that had her pictur."
They went on with their list.
The final blow to man's supremacy
Had been the acceptance of women in the military.
Overcome with the gloominess of the picture
They fell silent, each one letting his mind
Carry on into the darkening future.
The phone rang and Brayley turned to go in.
"I've got it" he said as he opened the screen door,
"Let's raise us some whiskers."

Independence

Pete Goodman was never able to keep a job
More than a few months at most.
Usually it was a matter of weeks.
The odd thing was that his employers
Were usually sorry to lose him.
He was a good workman and handy at anything,
But he could stand just so much bossing.
Then even mildly delivered requests
Stirred him to rebellion as much as downright orders.
He'd quit on the spot or not show up next day.
Rarely did arguments have any effect.
They usually brought forth more caustic rejoinders.
When Pete enlisted in the army for a three year term
About the time of the Spanish war
People in the village couldn't understand it.
Pete as a soldier didn't make sense.

They fully expected he'd be shot as a deserter
Before he'd been in a month.
Instead, when his first term ended,
He reenlisted for another three years.
When he was home on furlough once
One of his former short-term employers
Met him on the street.
He finally asked him how he stood army discipline.
"Did you ever throw down your gun and stamp your foot
And tell 'em to go to hell, when they gave an order?"
Peter looked at the speaker and then at the ground.
With the trace of a grin, almost in a whisper, he said:
"Once."

A Collector's Item

It was a beautiful day for the party,
Which was lucky since most of it was in the garden.
Mrs. Ardent would have plowed ahead in spite of bad signs
Since she had faith that, the affair being for a good cause,
The Lord would certainly be glad to assist.
Hand-painted posters aimed at the summer residents
Had been displayed generously up and down the valley.
They announced a "COLLECTOR'S FETE."
Not infrequently one villager would ask another
"Goin' t' see Mis' Ardent's feet?"
Mrs. Spencer Ardent had rented the Squire's estate
And had immediately stormed her way
Into the busy life of the summer colony.
She came endowed with an established social position
And was soon heartily accepted.
She was known in the village as a free spender.
She had brought several servants with her.
They were the first of a procession going and coming.
When Mrs. Ardent decided to have the fete
She was without a regular gardener and Lonzo Kilbrow
Was hired by the day to get the place in shape.
He was especially rushed as the affair grew in size.
Each person in the whole region was invited
To bring samples of his collecting hobby.

By the end of the second week Lonzo had found out
That he was not the only one whose pay was not forthcoming.
Worn out with the general hustle Lonzo lost his temper
When he again got nothing from Mrs. Ardent except promises.
He told her in no uncertain terms that he'd be there next day
And get what was due him or know the reason why.
The great affair was to be the next afternoon
And Mrs. Ardent was too rushed to stop to argue.
At the time for the opening, Alonzo in his working clothes
Was sitting on the front porch in a rocking chair.
Some looked shocked and some who knew him didn't see him.
When Miss Edmunds came along she greeted him cordially.
"Why Mr. Kilbrow, are you a collector too?"
Lonzo glanced toward the front door.
"Well t' tell the truth I'm callatin' to be one.
Wanted t' speak to th' hostess o' course
But th' hired girl said she couldn't see me."
He crossed his legs and settled back in the chair.
"I told her t' tell her missus she could see me
If she looked out here any time twixt now and dark."
A few minutes later a maid came out
And handed Lonzo an envelope.

A Stair Builder

After working along for some years as a carpenter
Henry found himself unexpectedly expanded.
He had become the village's first contractor.
For the first time a house was being built
According to blueprints from an architect's plans.
The dignity of the city planner might have suffered
If he'd known what most of the people called him.
They spoke of him as "that fool city architaker."
Hiram had once had some blueprint-reading experience
And he managed to get the new house going.
He was driven to despair by this employer
Who insisted on being on the job, right in the way,
And was forever changing the plans
Involving tearing down and rebuilding.

She also tried to hurry things in spite of the fact
That there were only a few men to be hired in the village
And materials had to be sent for out of town.
One hot summer day when she had been most trying
A stranger came along and offered his services.
He said he was a carpenter but his kit hadn't been shipped.
Anxious to get things done, Henry opened his own tool chest
And told the stranger to pick out what he'd need
To build some stairs to the cellar.
Assuring Henry that he was good at stairs,
The new man disappeared down below.
Henry was too busy to think of him again
Until an hour before quitting time he appeared.
Henry was surprised to find he was almost done with the stairs.
"Got one thing I want t' ask ye.
Do you want two little bits o' steps to the top
Er do you want one old heller?"

A Generous Soul

Whenever anything was going on in the village
Mrs. Humbert could be counted on to help.
In war or peace, whether it was providing for mind or body,
Mrs. Humbert's supply of enthusiasm was ready to gush.
When any outside organization sought funds—
"We understand your summer guests are most generous"—
It was Mrs. Humbert who went around with their solicitor.
Usually feeling somewhat beholden to the village
The first thing the summer resident knew
He had been picked by Mrs. H. as a "key person."
When the list of committees came out in the paper
He'd find he was heading one of them.
Later, consulting one of his committee he'd find
That membership had been accepted because Mrs. H. had said:
"You had been so enthusiastic about helping."
When time came for action it often happened
That the help Mrs. H. had so freely proffered herself
Was not forthcoming—she was out of town or unwell.
However she always continued to give oral help.

Her suggestions as to how others should carry on
Were freely and frequently given.
She could always suggest those from whom things could be borrowed.
If some lawn furniture were needed for the stage
In the performance the committee had been working on like mad,
Mrs. H. was sure if they call Mrs. Soandso
She'd be delighted to help them out.
"More dishes? Well, just call the Ladies Aid chairman."
A neighbor was praising Mrs. Humbert's many activities.
"But my lands" she concluded, "I never knew a body
So free and gen'rous with other folks' things."

Saving Grace

The posters for the auction had been put
On the space at the end of the church sheds.
Already the regulars had gone over the one
Hung up on the post by the stove in Brayley's store.
Uncle Sidney had taken it down to get it near enough
So his one good eye could take in the details.
His recollections of the Soper family
Were of gentle people who had made a real home
For three generations in the old farm house.
He recalled the parties he'd been to up there,
The kitchen dances and the candy pulls
And most of all the husking bees.
The old man even showed signs of a mild blush
When Silas Matthews recalled a certain girl
And a red ear of corn.
It was the passing of Miss Emily, the last of the line,
Which had brought about the auction.
She had run the place with an iron hand.
Nobody said she was unjust but few remembered her
For any acts of mercy or generosity.
Now her niece, who had visited her aunt once each summer,
Was busy getting things ready for the sale;
Throwing out innumerable useless savings,
And getting furniture moved down to the ground floor.
Many things most people would have thought hopeless

Had, over the generations, been stored in the attic.
There was broken crockery and worn out clothing
And every newspaper and magazine and catalog
That had come into the house for fifty years.
There were broken toys and rusty tinware under the eaves.
There was a large paper bag hanging from a rafter
Which the niece had supposed was filled with rags
Or perhaps pieces for a patchwork quilt.
She had bumped into it every time she went to the end of the attic.
Finally she yanked it down from its rusty nail.
A piece of cardboard was fastened to the string.
She took it to the window to read the faded letters.
Finally she made them out. They read:
"PIECES OF STRING TOO SHORT TO USE."

Time for Sleep

To all of the family, even to second cousins,
He was always known as "Uncle Ned."
The neighbors' children, who grew up playing around the house,
Called him "Uncle Ned" too.
He was the kind of man everybody would like
To claim as a relative.
He had never had any children of his own.
His only son had died with his mother at birth.
Perhaps because he hadn't any of his very own
To give his affection to
He had enough to spread around in a bigger circle.
In the summer the farmhouse was always full of visiting family.
As the years went by there were more and more
So that often there were three generations around the table.
Even when Uncle Ned was over eighty
He always looked forward to having the house full.
He'd often doze off in the midst of things
But he always insisted on being there.
His manner of getting folks off to bed
Had always been a joke in the family.
He'd wind the two clocks: the grandfather's one in the hall,

26

And the marbelized one on the living room mantel.
Then he'd go out onto the porch
And look at the thermometer and then the sky.
No matter what the outlook he'd always come in and say:
"It's a good night to sleep."
The summer he was eighty-five he slept much in his own room.
Then one morning they knew he would never waken.
That evening his favorite nephew
Stood on the porch trying to fit death into life.
Finally he turned toward the window
Of Uncle Ned's bedroom.
"Well Uncle Ned" he said
"It's a good night to sleep."

A Pig But No Pork

The Stevens place hadn't really been lived in
For the fifteen years before Miss Ellen died,
For she'd kept it all shut up except the kitchen wing.
As soon as the new family from the city bought it
They threw back the long-closed blinds
And opened the windows
To let in the sun-warmed air.
Folks walking past felt as though something pleasant
Had happened to them too.
Andrew Burton, the storekeeper, was the only one
Who had seen and talked to the new owners
When they moved in bag and baggage in the spring.
The children went to the village school
And through them news of the family was spread abroad.
They had let it be generally known
That they wished to become a part of the village life
And by fall they had been generally accepted.
They had a cow in the barn and had learned to milk it.
The hen house was populated with good stock
And from early summer there had been a pig in the pen
Back of the barn.
Andrew Burton, the storekeeper, had been their chief advisor

In matters economic, agricultural and even social.
One Sunday he was being shown around the place.
"That hog 'll be about right t' kill come cold weather" he said,
When they had arrived at the pen.
"That's what several of the men have said
But we've decided against it" the newcomer replied.
The storekeeper was plainly shocked at such unorthodoxy.
"No" the newcomer went on. "We've been at some pains
Bringing this creature up.
We are perfectly satisfied with it.
It seems utterly foolish to kill it
And then start in all over again."

A Binding Force

It seemed to the Professor that every year
When he came back to his small summer place
He heard about a new lawsuit Henry Dolliver was bringing.
It was generally over the lines of a piece of land
Between Henry's place and the Odburts' to the south.
The lower part, which was good meadow land,
Was plainly marked by a wall so there was no trouble there.
It was a stretch back on the hills, partly wooded,
Which was always causing trouble.
The Odburts would gladly have dropped the feud
But, when Henry cut some good logs on what they claimed,
They felt they had to stop him.
Then he'd dug up some old water rights
He claimed they had failed to recognize.
One morning Henry was walking down the road
Dressed in his best blue suit.
He met the Professor who taxed him with mistaking the day.
"Nope. I'm goin' t' Bennington acourtin' " he'd said.
The Professor going on to the store asked Brayley
About what Henry had told him.
"I supposed Henry Dolliver was a confirmed bachelor."
Learning that it was a matter of law and not of the heart
He asked about the land involved.

28

"Is there anything to make it so valuable?" he said.
"Nothin' but a rocky laydge" Brayley said.
"Not worth mentionin' really."
He stopped and then added:
"Oh I suppose it does help hold th' world t'gether."

Always Ready

"Every day like this un shortens th' winter."
Henry Peckham settled back in his chair
And thus spoke to the small group of regulars
Making the most of the late loafing weather
On the porch of Brayley's store.
Across the street Mrs. Brayley
Was taking up the geraniums from her flower bed.
Brayley said he'd been going over his diary.
This was the latest his wife had left her posies out
That he had on record except the year 1900.
Henry Peckham recalled that he couldn't remember a year
When they'd gone so late without setting up the stove
In their sitting room.
"My neighbor, she's had hern set up a month now.
Got her fall housecleanin' all done
And her winder curtains are all starched out.
I sez t' m' wife 'They look like little gals
All dressed up t' speak a piece.' "
He called attention to her now, raking leaves like mad
And putting them into the board enclosure to bank her house.
The calm quiet, which the waiting days of autumn
Brought to others, never affected her.
There were always things to be done no matter what.
"I'd hate t' live with anyone so pizen neat" Henry went on.
"Never go there but what I feel as if I orter
Take m' shoes off on the porch."
"Well I heard her say once" Brayley said as he turned to go in,
"That she never callated t' lay her head on her pillow
Without knowin' she'd left everythin' in dyin' order."

A Hot Spell

Even Deacon Stoddard, who was reputed
To wear his red flannels all summer,
Admitted it was "pretty warm."
The shades at the windows along the street
Were drawn down before the sun came up
To bottle up the night's refreshing coolness.
In the morning there was some activity
Around the store and postoffice
But soon after noon the deserted street
Shimmered in the scorching summer sun.
Brayley had moved his chair from the store porch
To a shady spot under the maple across the street.
He'd even taken off his black alpaca coat
And, with his chair tipped back,
He slept undisturbed.
Two small boys ambled along the highway
Savoring the hot dust with their bare feet.
The screen door of Brayley's slammed
And Brayley arose rubbing his eyes.
He hurried over to get two bottles of root beer
From the icy coolness of his refrigerator.
He returned to his chair but not to his nap.
The hot breeze brought the busy whirr of a mowing machine
And then the keen ring of a stone on a scythe.
A buckboard, sagging with the weight of Hen Sawyer,
Came slowly around the corner by the store.
He stopped by the hitching bar and Brayley got up,
This time taking his chair with him.
As he approached, Hen was wiping his brow with a blue handkerchief.
"Been a hot day if a feller was hayin' " he said—
"But I wa'n't."

Trial By Fire

Mrs. Mincote and her spinster daughter
Certainly had a good deal to put up with.
Not that Fred, the husband and father,
Wasn't a good provider and easy to get on with.
Between his periodic sprees he was all
That could be expected of a Mincote.
Even when he was on a bat he was usually quiet,
Spending most of his time in what served as his office
At the front corner of the horse barn.
His condition was most deplorable
When he'd suddenly decide to sober off.
Matters got worse and worse at those times
And no amount of dosing under the doctor's orders,
And given secretly, seemed to relieve his suffering.
Finally Etta saw a bath cabinet advertised—
A semi-turkish bath for the home.
It was a square affair in which the patient sat.
Inside there was a lamp which kept water boiling
From which the rising vapor enveloped the sitter—
All but his head which protruded through a hole in the top.
After much testimonial reading and letter writing
Etta and her mother took some of their egg money
And sent off a mail order for the cabinet.
Fortunately Fred wasn't around when it came
And he never saw it until he was recovering from another spree.
He was feeling unusually rocky this time
And his resistance was at a low ebb.
Even so it took the combined efforts of Etta and her mother
To get Fred securely installed within the cabinet.
The warm vapors rose to soothe his worn body
And he shut his eyes and drifted off to sleep.
Not long after, Etta and her mother, sitting on the porch,
Were brought up standing by a wild yell from the kitchen.
Out of the door streaked what looked like a small house
With a yelling head protruding from the roof,
And propelled rapidly by a pair of long hairy legs.
Smoke was pouring from under the contraption.
The inmate made for the watering trough and rolled into it.

Some days later the story reached the sitters at Brayley's store.
Brayley stopped with a sugar scoop in his hand.
"Well" he said, "if they's any curative prope'ties
In the much used threats of the fires of hell,
Mebbe Fred's womens' investment wa'n't hully lost."

Let 'em Set

While there were still signs of winter
Around clumps of bushes or on the north slopes
There was spring in the air.
The crows proclaimed it from the meadows.
Cattle, long winter-bound, cavorted with high-kicking awkwardness.
Kitchen doors along the road stood open
And the yards showed the collected rubbish of winter.
School children carried unwanted coats on their arms
As they raced toward the school yard.
A sailor was walking along the road toward the pass,
Through which the road crossed the mountains.
He carried a duffle bag on his shoulder.
His cap was shoved back on his head
And he whistled as he drank in the tonic of spring.
As a noisy pickup approached the sailor turned
And waited for it to come abreast.
A lank bearded figure opened the door with a broken glass.
He was still clad for below-zero weather
And his cap was pulled down over his ears.
The sailor threw his bag into the back and climbed in.
"Some day" he said with enthusiasm.
The driver nodded as he dropped in the chattering clutch.
Several times the sailor tried to make conversation
But the most he got was a reluctant nod or a grunt.
As the steaming car struggled over the summit and started down
The sun was shining on the tops of the peaks to the south.
The sailor leaned forward.
"What's the name of that peak?" he asked forgetting himself.
Looking straight ahead the driver said: "Dunno."
Twisting around in the seat the sailor tried again.
"What do they call this range we've just crossed?"

He got the same reply as before, spoken a bit more distinctly.
Evidently deciding this interrogation must be stopped
The driver, after a pause, said:
"We don't pay no attention t' them things.
We jest let 'em set there."

A Matchless Team

Mort always felt he had to have a "team o' hosses."
Not that he needed them for his small farm
For most of his work was teaming.
He drew logs or pulp wood in winter
Or ice during the short rushing ice-cutting season.
In summer he plowed gardens and then did haying.
Mort's various teams always had one common characteristic—
The two horses were never matched.
He seemed to have a positive genius
For getting horses that wouldn't work together
With any degree of efficiency.
If in the course of trading he ever did get a matched team
He was sure to trade one off in a short time.
Finally it got so he couldn't trade
Because nobody wanted either of his horses
And he didn't have any money to give to boot.
So he settled down with a rawboned bay
And a small faded blond mare with a crooked hind leg.
Owing to her infirmity the mare was always behind the bay.
When they tried to draw any sort of a load
They'd seesaw, first one pulling and then the other,
While Mort yelled directions and felt important.
He was plowing the Judge's garden one day
And the team was plodding along the furrow,
The mare a neck behind the big bay.
The Judge stopped to talk to Mort, remarking about the team.
Mort launched into biographical sketches of each member
And boasted of their abilities as a team.
"Seems as though that mare was always behind" the Judge said,
"If I was buyin' a team I'd get horses that pulled even."
Mort chewed a minute and then smiled indulgently at the Judge.

"Wal, I'll agree, on a straight pull it might be better
If the mare and th' bay were a mite evener in their pullin',
But yu see, Jedge, in my work I'm roundin' so many curves
That havin' 'em work this way makes out jest right."

The Siren's Call

In the good old days,
Which Ellery Stimson was sure had been the best,
The Undine fire engine had been famous.
It was a hand pumper of course.
Manned by a crew of such super-giants as Ellery had been,
The water-throwing power of old Undine
Had been something which won championships.
From all reports the chief object of the fire department
Was quite like that of a local baseball team.
It was a village-supported outfit which contended often
With rival water squirters from nearby towns
For the championship of the county or even the state.
Putting out fires, which were few and far between,
Was just the basic practical excuse for the red-shirt brigade.
They did cut quite a figure
As they drew the shining engine by a long rope
While the sun flashed from their brass speaking-trumpets
And made bright the patent leather on their helmets.
By the time Ellery was too old to man the pump
The company was disintegrating.
Of course Ellery thought it was another evidence
Of the decadence of the younger generation.
A few years later, when Ellery had passed his three score years,
The village was supporting a bright red motor outfit
Built for getting there fast and pumping efficiently
And, since the village had grown, it was often needed.
Naturally Ellery scorned the whole thing
But he especially hated the blood-congealing wailer
Which replaced the meeting-house bell as an alarm.
It was generally called a "sireen."
Ellery was sitting on the store porch one spring day
When the infernal silence-blaster started wailing.

34

A drummer came out of the store and looked up and down the street.
Spying Ellery he asked "What's that thing blowing for, a fire?"
Ellery looking completely disgusted, growled:
"Nope, th' fire's here already.
The damned thing 's bellerin' fer water."

A Pastoral Call

From any part of the upper road—
The one that follows the foothills—
You can hear the sound of running water.
There's the tumultuous sound of the spring-mad brook
And the steady roar of many waters from the mountain
And the friendly gurgling trickle beside the road
Where water is running into a mysterious hole.
All of the winter's snow back on the hills
Is rushing to get down into the valley.
Most of the farmhouses show signs of housecleaning.
Bedding bulges from upper windows
And parlor furniture adorns front porches.
Cattle are sunning themselves in barnyards,
Their rough winter coats already looking out of season.
In the sugar bushes at the foot of the mountain
The sun flashes from a hanging sap bucket.
Steam rolls out from the cracks in the weathered sugar house,
Having its few short weeks of glory.
When you get to the Burton place spring seems to end.
The big barn doors are shut and braced with poles.
The untrampled barnyard shows no sign of life.
The open shed is filled with shadow.
The only sign of life
Is the lazy wisp of between-meal woodsmoke
That drifts up from the kitchen chimney.
The Minister goes in at the kitchen door
Leaving his muddy rubbers on the porch.
Asa is lying in the bedroom off the kitchen
Where he's been lying for weeks and weeks.
The Minister tells Asa and his wife the village news.
Asa brightens up enough to hitch a bit of local history

To a name that's brought in.
The minister says something to Asa about getting well
Now that spring has come.
When Asa shakes his head the Minister tries to be comforting.
Asa looks at him with his fever-bright eyes.
"I don't mind goin', not a mite" he says in a throaty voice.
He settles down in the bed and speaks slowly.
"But I do kinda hate t' go .
In this dilapidated condition."

A Talking Tour

It was in the early days of motor touring.
The women in their wide-brimmed hats
Covered with veils wound around the neck,
Appeared to have bird cages for heads.
The men with visored caps and black goggles
Looked like large and baleful bugs.
The noisy speed of the new-fangled vehicle
And the enveloping and following clouds of dust
Added to the awesomness of its passage.
It was small wonder that horses took to trees
And quiet-loving country folk
Assigned the contraptions to the Devil.
It wasn't long, however, before the men
Got interested in how the devilish thing worked.
When one broke down, as it often did,
It was soon surrounded by eager eyes
Intent on seeing what was under the hood.
Often questions about directions brought about
Prolonged conversations involving history and local gossip.
Doctor Striker had been told that Vermonters
Were apt to be silent and hard to talk to.
However he'd found himself often involved for some time
When all he'd asked was a simple question.
So on his way back, since he was short of time,
He avoided any questionings until he came to a fork
After he'd come down the water-bar infested mountain road.
There was a faded sign but which way it pointed

He was unable to make out.
He saw a man coming along with a fishing pole
And as he drew near, the doctor asked:
"Is this the road to Bennington?" pointing to the right.
To his consternation, the man leaned against the car
And put his foot on the running board
As he started to give directions for travel.
Looking at him sternly the doctor said, speaking rapidly,
"Is this the road to Bennington?
Answer 'Yes' or 'No'."

An Error in Energy

It was a dull time in the village.
Winter was petering out and most of the winter jobs,
Such as getting in ice and wood, had been done.
It was too early to do anything about spring work
So the congregation around Brayley's stove
Was fairly large and steady in its attendance.
Rob Emerson casually remarked one day
That he wished he could get their piano moved upstairs.
There wasn't anybody to play it since his daughter had married
And it just stood in the sitting room taking up space.
Howard Duffy asked how Rob's cider was.
Rob opined he had a goodly supply on hand.
"Well" Howard said, "you furnish cider of the proper horsepower,
And I'll get me a crew t' move it up for yu."
He got a sheet of wrapping paper and a stub of a pencil.
After covering a lot of space with figures he announced
That if the cider was as stated, figuring the usual weight
Of a normal-sized piano, it would take four glasses per man
For four men to move the instrument up one flight.
The next night Howard and his three helpers were at Rob's door.
Having taken aboard the four glasses of cider each
As well as several of Mrs. Emerson's doughnuts,
They moved into the sitting room where the piano stood.
Mrs. Emerson closed the kitchen door
And went to work washing the glasses
And orderizing the kitchen.

She heard the heavy tread of the men as they moved into the hall.
With Howard shouting orders
And the others doing considerable grunting,
They moved onward and upward.
After what seemed a long time to Mrs. Emerson
They came down and went out the front door.
Rob came in and sat down by the kitchen table.
"What's th' matter?" she said, "Did yu strain yourself?"
"Nope. I didn't do no liftin' t' speak of."
"Well, what you so glum about. Piano's moved ain't it?"
Rob sighed. "We didn't figger suthin' right.
We was wrong on what a feller could do on four glasses o' cider."
Mrs. Emerson stood in front of her husband.
"What on earth you talkin' about. It's upstairs ain't it?"
Rob straightened up and fairly shouted:
"Upstairs? Hell, it's in the attic."

An Undelivered Letter

Because he had a good sized house and a wife who could cook
It gradually came about that Amos Goody kept boarders.
Amos found that it made it possible
For him to avoid a steady job in the sawmill.
He puttered around the house more and more
And as the number of woodsmen increased
Amos found his income sufficient to keep things going
And also to supply him with more and more liquid refreshment.
The fact that Sadie, his wife, had more and more to do
Didn't seem to bother Amos at all.
When she complained and asked for more conveniences
He put her off with promises.
One week in spring it had rained every day
So the men couldn't work in the woods.
They had hung around the house helping Amos
Dispose of another barrel of cider.
It was about as wet inside the house as it was out.
Toward the end of the week things got pretty thick.
Amos paid no heed to Sadie's complaints.
Then Sunday morning came and Amos was stunned

To find the kitchen empty and no fire built.
Sadie had walked out on him.
He knew she had gone down the valley to her mother's again.
He didn't dare to go to her and he couldn't write more than his name.
Finally one of the boarders agreed to write a letter
Which Amos could leave at her mother's door.
In it Amos told how he'd fix the kitchen sink
And put a new board over the hole in the porch.
He agreed to do all the things she'd been asking him to do
And even suggested other improvements.
As a clincher he swore he'd never drink another drop.
With shaky hand he signed his name.
The boarder addressed the envelope
And putting on his cap Amos went out the door.
He stopped on the porch and peered down the road.
Sure enough that was Sadie plodding along with a handbag in her hand.
Amos turned and went back into the kitchen.
He tore the letter up and dropped it into the stove.
He got back to the door just as Sadie
Was coming up the step with a hole in it.
Amos stood looking at her, barring the door.
"Well" he said, "What in hell 's brought you back here?"

Old Cream Pot

Alfred Starks had to admit to his wife
That when he'd traded that old brindle for the black and white
He'd been taken in by appearances.
Of course she did give a good quantity of milk as promised
But it was very decidedly lacking in cream content.
So when Israel Judson dropped in on his way from the creamery
And let fall that he might be in the market for a cow or two
Alfred immediately thought of the black and white.
He also recalled a deal he'd had some years before
When Israel had got the better of him—
A recollection which added zest to the occasion.
By the time they had got down to dollars and cents
Alfred had Israel all set to buy the black and white.
Her obvious ability as a producer of milk

39

Had evidently appealed to him as it had to Alfred.
Twice Israel raised his offer but Alfred shook his head.
His price was still two five-dollar notches above Israel's bid.
While Israel hesitated and looked, Alfred went to the house.
Said he'd had codfish for breakfast and was awful dry.
When Alfred came out Israel was looking over another cow.
Just then the kitchen door opened and Mrs. Starks shouted:
"Alfred Starks, don't you dare sell old Cream Pot. Ye hear!"
"You go on in and ten t' yer own business" Alfred answered.
As she slammed the door Israel wanted to know which was "Old Cream
    Pot?"
"O, she's that black and white. Don't know what she's talkin' 'bout."
In less than ten minutes Israel was driving out leading "Cream Pot"
And Alfred was tucking the extra ten into his wallet.
His wife came out on the porch, holding her hand out.
"I'll take five dollars o' that money" she said.
"Salary fer actin' and takin' your sassy remarks
Without talkin' back."

Something Missing

Standing in the road where the bus had dropped him
Ira gazed up the hill where a winding road climbed.
He could hardly believe he'd landed at the right spot.
He remembered a few trees along the wall that held the road
But now, except where it looped into the meadow,
The whole road was hidden by trees.
All he could see of the farmhouse was one end of the roof
And the kitchen chimney from which smoke was drifting.
As he went up the road he noticed
That it wasn't half as steep as he'd remembered it.
And that rock out in the meadow—
Well of course it might have weathered away with the years.
They'd always called it "Big Rock."
The apple orchard too had shrunk
Even though the trees were years older.
He hoped the present owner would have a few of those apples
So he could show the fellows in the office
Why he was always talking about the fruit his father raised.

40

A week later Ira was back at his office desk.
In spite of some outdoor color on his cheeks
He looked older and he was much quieter.
For years he'd been telling the various young folks
Who moved in and out of the office
About the terribly steep hill he used to slide on
In front of the farmhouse.
They all knew about the enormous rock near the turn
And especially they knew of the wonderful big apples.
When he'd come back from his visit
They'd gathered around his desk to hear how things looked
After forty-odd years absence.
One asked about the hill and another about the big rock.
And others remembered those wonderful apple trees.
Some of the older ones realized
That a change had come over Ira.
He seemed to have lost something.
At first he spoke with some of his old enthusiasm,
But it only lasted a few minutes.
"Yes" he said finally, with a faraway look in his eyes,
"The hill was there, and the rock was there,
And the apple trees—they were all there."
He stopped and fingered something on his desk:
Then he added, almost in a whisper:
"But the boy wasn't."

Too Much To Expect

Rollin had been trying to get to his woodlot
Ever since there had been enough snow for sledding.
At last the day had come when the winter road was open
And the prospects for a good day were bright.
He got up long before daylight and lit the kitchen fire.
Then he went out and fed his horse and the cows.
When he came in his wife had breakfast ready—
Fried salt pork and potatoes and a steaming pot of coffee.
She had his lunch put up in a pail
And, when Rollin tucked it under the hay for the horse,
He felt of the jug of cider he'd smuggled in.

By the time the sun came over the mountain
Rollin was well up on the road.
He had on his worn buffalo coat
With an old surcingle around it for a belt.
He had a red handkerchief tied outside of the turned-up collar.
His frosty breath made icicles on his whiskers.
About nine Rollin turned off the broken road.
A smooth white stretch, a little wider than the sled,
With trees on either side showed the way to the woodlot.
He soon emerged into the clearing where he'd cut the year before.
He took off the mare's bridle and tied her halter to a tree.
He gave her the hay and picked up the cider jug.
He had to tip it quite a bit more
Than he did when he'd started up the mountain.
He ate a little of his lunch and then hung his coat on a bush.
He was ready for the day's chopping.
Later, when he came into the kitchen,
His wife looked up from putting something into the oven.
"Well good lands!" she said, looking at the clock,
"What on earth fetched you back now?
You couldn't 'a more 'n got up there and come back,
Let alone doin' any choppin'."
Rollin sat down in the corner and pulled his moccasin rubbers off.
"Had a mite o' hard luck" he mumbled.
"Matter of fact I forgot m' axe."
His wife was stunned to silence for only a minute.
Finally she ran out of words and breath and turned away.
Rollin hung his mittens on a line over the stove.
"Gosh a' mighty" he said, "y' can't expect a feller
T' remember everythin'."

For Whom Did The Bell Toll?

For over a century the red brick church
Had stood a stalwart sentinel on the hill.
It's supporters had grown fewer and fewer
Until it was closed much of the time,
Since there was no longer a settled minister.
Then a group of summer residents began to take an interest.

Arrangements were made for a summer supply
And a meeting was called of all those interested
To make arrangements for the opening service.
One of the older members suggested that the old custom
Of ringing the bell an hour before service,
So it could send its invitation up and down the valley,
Be revived, as well as having it tolled
As the minister mounted to the pulpit.
He was deeply moved as he spoke of what that bell had meant
For many years in the life of the village.
The idea was taken up with such enthusiasm
That few noticed elderly Miss Cutler's evident dissent.
She sat on the edge of her chair shaking her head
And trying to attract the attention of the moderator.
Finally someone sitting next obtained a hearing for her.
She arose with some difficulty and her voice trembled
As she told the silent group why she couldn't stand it
If they ever tolled that old bell again.
"The last time that bell was tolled
Was on the occasion of the death of our beloved President,
Our dear Calvin Coolidge."
She faltered and then went on.
"I shall never forget that day
Of tragic loss to our country.
I just couldn't bear to hear that solemn sound again."
She turned to find her chair.
As she sat down she said in a stronger voice;
"Or mebbe it was President Harding."

Incriminating Evidence

When Miss Estelle Honeywell bought the old Hanson place
She seemed to have two objects in view.
In saving the fine example of colonial architecture
She was, she felt, continuing something
Of the staunch New England character.
Then too she wanted to improve the life of the village.
She never thought it was right to spend money
Unless she could thereby improve humanity.

She had succeeded in restoring the simple beauty of the house,
But her contacts with local labor had not resulted
In any great success in the way of standard raising.
She found she could not change local working habits to suit herself.
Any success she had was soon found to be simply on-the-job reformation,
When she happened to be in sight.
She had early suspected that Billy Emdsen, who did work
Mostly on the lawns and flower gardens,
Was given to strong drink.
Not that she had ever seen real proof of overindulgence;
It was his very red face and laughing good nature
Which were her chief grounds for suspicion.
One Monday morning she had been talking about the garden.
Then she said: "I hope, Mr. Emdsen, that you are not a drinking man."
Billy straightened up and smiled at her.
"Why Mis' Honeywell, what 'd ever make you think
That a pale-face like me was a drinker of hard likker?"
Sure she was right from this evasion, she went on.
"I happen to know that you spent all of Saturday afternoon in the Tavern."
"Well now, what makes you say that, Mis' Honeywell?"
"Your newly-painted wheelbarrow gave you away," she said.
"It stood outside all of the afternoon."
The next morning when the maid brought her breakfast in
Miss Honeywell told her to have Mr. Emsden come to the door
As soon as he appeared.
"It's funny, Miss Honeywell" the maid said,
"Nobody 's seen him, but his wheelbarrow 's standing outside
And the chauffeur says it's been there all night."

Spread Too Thin

Giles Summers had held about every town office.
He'd been assistant Constable when he was twenty-one
And soon after that he was Deputy Sheriff.
He'd run for Sheriff several times
But, while he carried the town, he couldn't carry the county.
After being Road Commissioner three years
He'd got enough voters down on him,
Because the road in front of their places wasn't fixed,

44

To lose in the next town meeting.
A few years later he was elected Selectman over his neighbor Stevens
Who never spoke a civil word to him afterward.
Because he always attended the caucus
He was usually on the Republican Town Committee.
In due time he went to the state legislature as representative.
He had very good committee appointments
And in general made a reputation for himself.
About then the party leaders were looking around
For some man to elect to state office.
Their section had been neglected for some years.
They decided Giles was known more than anybody else
In other sections of the state so they picked him out.
They sent a couple of men to the village from the county seat
To find out how Giles stood in his own town.
They asked Uncle Tom Howard, one of the oldest citizens,
What he thought of Giles for Lieutenant Governor.
Uncle Tom rubbed his hands together and looked at the ceiling.
"Well, Giles has worked up and in gen'al he's done his work well.
Showed up pretty good up to Montpelier I hear too.
But Lieutenant Governor—I dunno.
I'm afraid, come t' spread him out all over th' state,
He'd make an awful thin coatin'."

No Snacks

Etta Larch had been ailing for some weeks,
But she wasn't any hand to give up to things
So she kept going until she was downright sick.
Charles, her bachelor brother, and her sister
At last held a consultation and called the doctor.
He found Etta in the kitchen
Sitting by the stove dozing, mending in hand.
She tried to spruce up when she saw the doctor
And said there really wasn't any need.
However she soon found herself in bed
And a trained nurse lording it over her.
When Charles came in toward noon
He found he'd been dislodged from his downstairs bedroom

And his clothes were up in a long-unused room upstairs.
He didn't say anything but he couldn't remember a night
When he hadn't slept in that downstairs bedroom.
That night he stumbled up the stairs to his new room
Feeling rather sorrier for himself than for his sister.
Tight-shut shutters had kept daylight out of the new room
For many many years, and they were still shut.
The next morning Charlie's sister, Elmira, told the hired man
That Charles was worn out and they'd let him sleep.
So for the first time in fifty years or more
Charles slept while the new day came in
And, when the sun climbed above the woods beyond the pasture,
He was snoring peacefully in the dark chamber.
Finally soon after the clock had struck nine
He clumped down the stairs and hurried toward the sink,
Rubbing his eyes as he tried to focus on the clock.
By the time he had washed the sticks from his eyes
He was expressing his opinion of those who had let him sleep.
He didn't even ask for his sick sister.
He ignored the breakfast Elmira was putting on the table.
"Not by a durned sight" he said as he struggled into his jumper.
"It's three hours past breakfast time
And dinner time 's three hours off."
He slapped his faded felt onto his head
And opened the door.
"I ain't ever et between meals" he said over his departing shoulder,
"And by mighty, I don't cal'late t' commence now."

Holmes Andrus: Auctioneer

"Going . . . . Going . . . . "
How many thousands of times those words
Were the warning that you'd better raise your bid
Or give up getting the thing you wanted.
Think of the innumerable possessions
Which often had been accumulated by generations
That he pronounced those words over.
"Going . . . . Going . . . . "

Prized possessions that had meant days of hard work;
Hand-made things into which family affection had been woven.
These he would handle with knowing care
For many times he knew the story.
When the sale started with the groups of little things,
With the price going up in five cent bids,
You wondered how he'd get to anything worth while.
He seemed to know that these bits of dented kitchenware
And the odd forks and knives might help to start a home.
So he took pains with them as he felt out his audience.
Now and then, as the day wore on, he'd stop the bidding
To ask the folks on the outskirts please to put off their visiting
So he wouldn't miss anyone who wanted to make a bid.
"Going . . . . Going . . . . . Are you all done?"
Still another chance, but time was moving on.
Think of the hundreds of tools, gadgets, utensils,
Many of them of another day and generation,
That he had to know the names of and their uses.
He had to know cattle and horses and harvested crops
And whether to push the bidding higher or cry "Sold."
He knew antiques, from delicate pieces of glass to colonial highboys.
He knew the dealers too and what each wanted most.
He had to know, most of all, people.
He not only knew them but he liked them—all kinds.
He knew who'd take a joke and when to spring it.
He wove with a thread of understanding
And drew his audience into his friendly circle.
You wondered at his unwearied enthusiasm.
His good nature never seemed to wear thin
No matter how long the day or how trying.
"Going . . . . Going . . . . "
Day after day, week after week, year after year
Thousands have heard him say it.
Now it is they who say the last word,
Gratefully remembering:
"Gone."

One Swear Not Enough

John Slocum kept a small store near the depot.
He carried about everything anyone might need.
Food and raiment was mixed in with hardware, tools, and paints.
In the shed at the back he kept grain.
His books contained almost a complete roll
Of the inhabitants of the valley
And some from over the mountain.
John was also postmaster and that meant
He carried the mail across to the depot.
He kept a cow at home which he cared for
Until the boys were old enough to milk.
He'd held several town offices
But one he liked the best he held the longest.
He liked the intricacies of the law
And being Justice of the Peace suited him exactly.
He liked to read the statutes
And he had a pretty good working knowledge of them.
When he held court, even in his back room,
He conducted the trials with real dignity.
One time Hi Clifford had been summoned to appear before him.
He was accused by his neighbor, Thomas Snow,
Of allowing his chickens to trespass on the Snow domains.
Hi was duly sworn and started testifying.
Suddenly Tom Snow let his chair down with a bang.
He interrupted the solemn proceedings.
"Swear him again, John, swear him again," he shouted.
"He's lyin' like hell."

Lengthening His Days

When he got so it was hard for him to walk
Grandfather took over churning the butter.
He wore a big checked and faded blue apron
When he was working in the addition off the kitchen
Which had been made into a creamery.
The butter that was turned out there
Was as good as any turned out anywhere.

48

As Grandfather got lamer
Even the churning made him do considerable complaining
About how hard work it was.
His son often urged him to give it up.
He could have done it much easier himself
But Grandfather wouldn't hear to it even if he did complain.
The big barrel churn had a clamped-on lid
And every now and then—
There was much red-faced argument as to the cause—
The cover would drop off and out would go the butter.
Grandfather was always set certain it wasn't anything he'd done
Or neglected to do that caused the disaster.
Being a deacon of the church all he could say was:
"Jerusha Jane Hosiphat," which somehow didn't seem adequate.
One hot day he'd finished churning
And apron and all he was sitting on the porch cooling off.
"Tired, Father?" his daughter asked.
He shook his head and puffed out his cheeks.
"You know if I had only an hour to live what I'd do?"
He looked at his daughter and smiled.
"I'd go to churnin'. Never knew time t' stretch out so long
As it does when I'm churnin'."

Poor Fare

Mrs. Ballard put a fresh stick into the stove
And opened the pipe damper.
She hurried into the butt'ry and out to the table,
Carrying this and that in the way of food.
She hurried into the dining room
And spread a red tablecloth on the oak table.
Every few minutes she rushed at the stove
Where steam was spouting from various vessels.
That morning her husband had told her that the man,
Who had bought the next farm for a summer home,
Was coming out to look things over.
He'd asked if it would inconvenience them
To take him in for dinner and of course he'd told him to come.
Mrs. Ballard had to admit that he couldn't do less

But it did seem as though she'd never had less to offer.
There was a stomping on the porch
And Mr. Ballard led the new neighbor in.
Mrs. Ballard wiped her hand on her apron and shook hands.
"I'm sure you're welcome but you'll have to put up
With whatever we happen to have."
The new neighbor apologized for putting her out
And assured her that she was not to do anything extra.
Mr. Ballard took him to the sink to wash.
Mrs. Ballard opened the oven disclosing a pan of bulging biscuits.
"This war flour is so awful I just worked up a batch of biscuits.
They don't look jest right but they'll have to do."
She put a big lump of butter into the mashed potato
And added more butter to the corn—"some we canned ourselves."
Seated at the table Mrs. Ballard hovered about
Passing this and that, always with an apology.
At last there were two pies, apple and cherry,
With plenty of rich cream to pour over them.
As he was leaving, the over-stuffed neighbor
Was expressing his thanks and still trying
To make Mrs. Ballard accept something for the wonderful meal.
"I wouldn't think of chargin' a neighbor for a meal o' vittels"
She said, rolling her hands up in her apron.
"Certainly not th' kind I had t' set out t'day.
Let me know when you're comin' next time,
And I'll try t' get somethin' fit t' eat"
She called as he went down the steps.

Beyond

During most of the fifty years of his life
Charlie Pease had stayed in his valley.
Once, when he was a young fellow, he went to Boston
And, if the illness of his best heifer hadn't called him back,
He'd have gone on to the World's Fair at Chicago.
He'd been over the East Mountain several times
And he had been disappointed to find
That all he saw to the east, even in that valley,
Were more mountain barriers shutting him off.

As time went on he began to talk
About wanting to get out of his valley.
All his life he'd really been restless—
He wanted to see what was behind those mountains.
From what he'd heard he thought when he got to the ocean
And could get an uninterrupted view
Clean off into measureless space,
Then he'd feel he'd seen all there was to see.
So when his son suggested he ride across New Hampshire
In his car clear to the seacoast,
He made up his mind he'd go, chores or no chores.
They got to the shore in time to see the sunset,
And they stayed up late enough to see the moon rise.
Charlie gazed and gazed.
When anyone tried to talk to him he shook his head.
For once words failed him.
He spent the next day watching the heaving water
And looking off to the misty horizon.
By the end of the second day he showed signs of a return to normal.
"B'mighty" he said, "All m' life I've hankered
T' look so fur there wa'n't nothin' more t' see.
Mountains surroundin' allays makes a feller
Oneasy t' know what's on th' other side.
But here they ain't one tarnation thing in th' way."
"So you think now you can rest easy, do you, Father?" his son asked.
Charlie sighed and shifted his gaze.
"Why yes—yes, I guess I'd orter."
He took off his hat and scratched his head
"But I just got t' wonderin' sort of.
What d' you 'spose they is out beyond that line
Where them ships pop up now and again?"

A Legal Prop

If Henry Stoddard hadn't helped at the Day auction
His life might have gone on the even tenor of its way.
But there, after everything had been sold,
Henry had rescued from a discarded box a book.
It was old and leather-bound and looked impressive

So Henry carried it home.
It turned out to be a law book for laymen.
Henry wasn't much of a reader
And he never did make much sense out of the book.
Nevertheless the knowledge that all that legal lore
Was stored on the shelf back of his sitting room stove,
Gave Henry a feeling of confidence.
He usually did most of his not inconsiderable loafing
In and around George Wissell's blacksmith shop.
He had usually been a listener during the numerous arguments
That flourished, especially around town meeting time.
He rarely ventured an opinion—until he got his law book.
After that he got so he'd drop in a bit of legal lore
Which was usually accepted without comment.
He was careful of his audience, being especially wary
Of saying anything when George Wissell, the smith, was listening.
One day there was a discussion of the duties of a Selectman.
Thinking Wissell was occupied with his work
Henry offered a few words of wisdom
And the discussion quieted down.
"That's the right of it, no ifs, ands or buts" Henry had said.
George Wissell thrust a hot shoe into the water tub.
"How come you know that's the right of it?" he asked Henry.
Startled at finding George had overheard, Henry hesitated.
"What's that you said, George?" he asked, sparring for time.
George repeated his question.
"How do I know? Well I'll tell ye.
I got me a law book to home; that's how I know."
George started pumping the bellows.
"I got a vi'lin over t' my place" he said,
"But I can't play it."

A Reasonable Facsimile

Nobody knew whether Miles King's shiftlessness
Was really a burden to his sister Sarah or not.
She frequently alluded to it in public
But she always made a joke of it.
She was too even-tempered to get upset

By the way things looked around the place.
Inside she kept things in comfortable disorder.
She always appeared in public neatly dressed
And, when she drove to church or to some social affair,
She never looked as though she belonged in her conveyance.
It was a buggy, always looking muddy, and full of rattles.
Miles, sitting beside her, looked much as the buggy did.
But it never seemed to worry Sarah.
She might make some joking remark to her hostess,
As Miles whipped up the bony horse and rattled off,
But it was always in a tone of affectionate banter.
She understood why he was that way about externals
And she knew what he was beneath his skin.
One day a neighbor was sitting on Sarah's porch
When Miles drove the cows past to the barn.
The neighbor remarked that she didn't see
That large black and white cow they'd had for some time.
"O, Miles went and sold her" Sarah said with a sigh.
"I'm sorry too; it was the best cow we had—
That is" she added looking up from her mending,
"She looked more like a real cow
Than anything else we ever had."

Immortal Opposition

Whenever any movement was on foot in the valley
When popular support was being sought,
Everyone knew where Caleb Hartwell would stand.
He had an uncanny ability to sense popular trends
And an unswerving habit of getting on the off-side.
There was never any likelihood of unanimous action on anything
As long as Caleb was able to register his opinion.
By the time he was middle-aged
He had had or was having a row with everybody in the valley.
The only people he got on with
Were those who never had any opinions about anything.
As a young man he had joined the Grange and then the Lodge.
He'd stayed in each only a short time
And then had left in a cloud of smoke

53

And the smell of something scorching.
Each new minister tried to get Caleb to church.
If he succeeded once it was enough.
Caleb's criticisms lasted throughout the pastorate.
One winter the news got around
That Caleb was seriously sick with pneumonia.
His dislike of any of the available doctors
Had made him keep up until he was practically helpless.
In less than a week the rural mail carrier brought the news
Down to the village store that Caleb had passed on.
"When 'd he die?" the storekeeper asked.
"Just before I got to the house; 'bout an hour ago."
The storekeeper put a bolt of calico back on the shelf.
"Well" he said turning around, "I don't know where Caleb's gone
But by now he's in a tarnation row with somebody."

Behind the Barn

When Ezra Hopkins' barn burned
Fortunately the stock were in the night pasture
And he had only just begun his haying.
What bothered Ezra as much as the loss
Was the stark staring fact that now
He'd have to do the thing he'd always had in the back of his mind
As the ultimate luxury he'd someday indulge in.
Every discomfort he'd had to put up with
And every new convenience he'd wanted and often needed,
He'd put on one side with: "When I build me m' new barn."
Now the dream would have to become a reality.
To make it handier he built the new barn
Right across the road from the house.

By the time Ezra had become so crippled with rheumatizm
That he had to give up and move to the village,
The barn, weathered to a silver gray, was still the "new barn."
The real estate agent had brought a man to see the place
And Ezra had been pointing out lines with his cane.
Sitting on the kitchen porch the man asked Ezra
About the water supply and the sugar bush.

Finally after hearing much of the history of the place
The man turned to the agent and said:
"Well Mr. Edgerton, I guess this is the place we want,
Can we go down now to your office and draw up the papers?"
Ezra was stunned at the speed of the decision.
He was more stunned when they got up to go.
Pointing to the "new barn" the stranger said:
"The first job will be to tear down that old barn there."
Ezra stared at the man thinking he had misunderstood.
"Tear that barn down?" he said.
"Why that's the best buildin' on th' place.
I built that barn m' self not more 'n thirty years ago."
The man was looking off at the hills.
"No. I cannot have that building there."
Still incredulous Ezra persisted.
"But I put it there apuppose to have it handy to the house."
He looked with affection at the building whose every timber he knew.
"Just why 'd you want t' tear m' barn down? Tell me that."
The buyer smiled indulgently.
"Well Mr. Hopkins, I'm sorry, but it ruins the view."
Ezra snorted. "View? View! Well let me tell ye,
There ain't one damned thing behind that barn
But some mountains."

A Mitigating Circumstance

Of course during the two years
The young minister had stayed in the village
He had not escaped some criticism.
Being the successor to Dr. Anderson,
Who had served the church for forty-odd years,
It was natural that some of the older members
Found a stranger in the pulpit hard to bear.
However the young minister—and he was usually called that—
Was very tactful and made his changes slowly.
Gradually the empty pews began to be filled.
By the end of his second year the church was done over
And at that time several relics of the past
Disappeared, especially some portraits

From the "Ladies Parlor" in the basement of the church.
This aroused the ire of Deacon Elmer.
He was only mollified when the young minister
Explained how unworthy of these fathers in Israel
The crayon portraits really were.
The Deacon immediately made arrangements for an oil of himself
To be made from special photographs after his demise
By adding a codicil to his will.
When it was reported that the young minister
Had received a call to a much larger church
There was a feeling of sorrow all over the village.
Only Deacon Elmer failed to express regret.
He kept a tight-mouthed silence
And people generally thought it was the picture episode
Which still rankled in his bosom.
Finally Ned Stiles said to the Deacon
That he just couldn't understand his attitude.
"Some say you're even glad he's going" Ned said.
The Deacon was silent for a minute, then he said:
"No, that ain't it at all.
I'm sorry he's goin' but they's another side to it.
He's brought our church suthin' of an honor
It ain't never had before."
He shut his mouth tight and looked at Ned.
"Did you ever stop t' think that he's th' first minister
Our church ever had, t' my knowledge,
That anybody else wanted?"

A Tale of a Pig

Mrs. Anita Belmont had lived in her new home
Only one summer.
She had bought the Aiken place one fall
And had it made over during the winter.
She had left the old barn with its sag
Because it was picturesque, only adding a coat of red paint.
When she had come up in the spring
A problem at once presented itself.
She found that the young man who had collected her garbage

56

Had been drafted and had gone off to war.
She finally consulted the Farm Bureau agent in the village
About her need for a garbage remover.
"Well, Miss Belmont, as I recall it
You still have the old hog pen back of the barn, haven't you?"
She reported it still stood there
But that it had been thoroughly cleaned and painted.
"Well why not buy a little pig, Miss Belmont?
Feed what 's edible, for a hog, to it,
Add a little grain perhaps,
And in the autumn you'll have quite a respectable hog.
Be helping with the food supply too."
Following his advice a small pig was duly installed in the pen.
There was considerable company at Miss Belmont's
And the cook liked the guest back of the barn
So the supply of pork grew daily.
Late that fall Miss Belmont again called the Farm Agent.
She was going back to the city and what should she do
With the good-sized pig in her pen.
The Agent told her he knew of a nearby farmer
Who might be interested and that he would call him up.
In due time the farmer presented himself at Miss Belmont's.
He looked the pig over.
"Good lookin' hog" he said,
"How much you cal'latin' he ought t' fetch?"
Miss Belmont said: "Well, my goodness,
I hate to part with the little creature at any price.
However, I must.
Let me see now. I paid ten dollars for him
When he was a baby. Let me see—
Of course we've had the use of him all summer.
Would you think five dollars would be too much now?"

Giving Nature a Chance

Probably Doctor March was better known
Than any other doctor in the County.
It wasn't that he knew more medicine than the others;
It was the rarity of the cult he followed

Which brought him fame.
He was an "Eclectic" and there were many to testify
To his skill in the use of native herbs.
He drove over the country in a high buggy
Always sitting on the edge of the seat
And always looking at something far beyond.
Now and then he would pump on the reins or speak to the horse,
But he paid no attention to those he met on his way.
When he talked he made a putt-putting noise
Puffing out his lips which looked very red
Against the white of his long beard.
In 1917 the other two doctors in the village enlisted.
They were both young and one of them
Was very free in expressing his scorn for the old Doctor.
The first day he had acquired a uniform
He was showing himself off near the post office
When Doctor March came out in a hurry as usual
And looking neither to the right or left.
The young doctor stopped almost in front of him.
"Well Doctor" he said in a condescending tone,
"What's going to happen to the town now
With both us young doctors going off to war;
What'll folks do?"
Dr. March putt-putted and pulled his beard.
"Well I imagine considerable more of 'em—putt—putt—
Will die—putt—putt—a natural death."

In Wartime

The mellow wind bent the grass making a light green wave
That billowed along the hill toward the brook.
Under an elm, black and white cows stood.
Birds flew here and there.
Their songs made ripples in the flowing rustle of the leaves.
Across the valley there was a farmhouse,
And a gray barn and a leaning silo.
Bush-covered stone walls hid the road
That climbed the hill slantwise to get a better footing.
There was a row of maples near the farmhouse—

58

Fulfilled promises made to some thoughtful forebear,
Long since done with promises and planting.
Meadows, pastures, plowed land with brush division lines;
And cloud shadows drifting over all the precise patterns,
Paying no heed to fences or earth's ideas of order.
Up the slope the gray shadows crept
To fade against the green wall of mountain.
All the sounds were gentle,
Each fitting in to make silence into sound
Without robbing silence.
The smooth pastures curved to the green hills
Which took them to the mothering serenity of the mountain.
Peace lured the soul.
How to be a part of this tranquil pattern,
How to hold forever this elemental peace,
And still not be a tree or grass or four-footed beast!

A Scarecrow De Luxe

When the Doctor had started out
He had planned to hang an old shirt on a lath cross
And top it with an old fishing hat.
Somehow the whole thing got away from him.
He found himself doing something he'd wanted to do
Ever since he'd been a boy on the farm.
He'd never been satisfied with the scarecrows his father made.
He'd never been allowed to use the necessary clothes
To make something that really looked like a man.
So when he decided his few rows of corn
Warranted the guardianship of a scarecrow
He discovered that here was a chance
To satisfy his thwarted ambitions.
He discarded the simple one he'd thought of
And spent several hours making a realistic work of art.
He used an old suit of course
Though he felt sure his wife would think it too good.
In the midst of his creative effort his wife had called
That there were patients waiting in his office.
She had wondered what he was spending so much time on in the barn.

The next morning he set his masterpiece up in the garden,
Where Jim Hanley was to work that day.
The Doctor saw Jim go past the window.
Before he'd had time to finish his last cup of coffee,
Jim was asking for him at the kitchen door.
"I just come t' say I'm quittin' " he said through the screen door.
He'd worked there so long the Doctor thought
This was some sort of a joke at first.
But Jim insisted it wasn't just for the day—he was through for good.
"Nope, Doc, I'm sorry but it's against m' principles."
Still thinking it was a joke the Doctor remarked
That he didn't know Jim had any such embellishments as principles.
"Nope, I'm honest 'bout this, it's jest too much t' bear.
I can't work for no man that's got a scarecrow
That's better dressed than I be; that's all."

Rest for the Weary

It had been a tough winter for everybody.
Snow had fallen in early December
And kept piling up week after week.
Even the usual January thaw had made little impression
Though it had made the going about impossible.
Dr. Mosely had been run ragged.
He generally kept a single horse
As a sort of spare when his team was overworked.
Jim Vetal was his driver and general assistant.
This winter he had to hire a team from the livery stable
Several times to give the Doctor's horses a rest.
But there was no rest for the Doctor.
One night in late February Jim was letting the team walk
As they came into the village street.
The worn Doctor was asleep on the seat beside him.
He suddenly came to and told Jim
To let him out at the Holland's house.
He would walk the little way from there.
Mrs. Holland had been very sick for some weeks.
She'd seemed better that morning when he stopped
But he'd sleep better if he stopped in just for a minute.

60

Mrs. Holland was a large woman and very well upholstered.
As the Doctor came into the room he noticed
That her breathing certainly was much better.
He felt her pulse, holding his worn silver watch.
Then he said he'd just listen to her heart a minute.
There were no such things in those days
As stethoscopes or any mechanical hearing aids.
The physician got his knowledge first hand.
So he pressed his ear over Mrs. Holland's heart.
He told her to start counting slowly
And not to stop until he told her.
She started—"one—two—three—four—five————"
The tired Doctor found himself in a comfortable position
Sitting in a low chair with his head on a soft warm pillow.
He heard "twenty-six—twenty-seven————"
Then off in the distance he heard a voice:
"Five thousand seven hundred and fifty-two,
Five thousand seven hundred and fif————"
The Hollands could never say enough
In praise of Dr. Mosely.
Worn out as he had been he had sat up half the night
To make sure of the safety of his patient.

On Memorial Day

The sun rose slowly
Over the edge of the east mountains.
It dissolved the morning mist
Which had hidden the rows of stones.
It caught the shining particles in the granite
And made whiter the marble stones against the fresh green.
From the still misty curtain along the brook
Came the songs of many birds
And the sound of running water.
Gradually as he looked and listened
There came to him a feeling of life
In that place where only the dead dwell.
He thought of some of the people he'd known;
His own family—two generations—

He could call to mind how they looked
And even hear again the sound of some of the voices.
Back in the "old part" were the stones of those he'd never known
Except as names in the family Bible
Or as some trait, some special characteristic,
Had been handed down from generation to generation.
And so it was with all the people there
Whose names were carved on the stones:
They were each one a real part of the living present.
To the living, who would come to that spot
On this special day of remembrance,
Had come something which lived on
From generation to generation.
Something passed on to be woven into the warp and woof
Of new and ever-changing times.
Things worthy and things unworthy;
Things that helped and things that hindered;
Talents hidden in a napkin of obscurity
Which chance unfolded in another generation.
There he stood in the midst of a world that had been
But which was a part of the living present
As it would be of the days yet to come.
Here indeed was life immortal.

She Hung On Her Words

In spite of the fact that most people
Felt the loss of him to be an addition to the place,
When Hen Dilt was found—
A piece of permanently suspended animation
In the attic of the old Dilt house—
Not a hint of anything but real sympathy
Came to the long-suffering sister with whom he had lived.
Never in the long years of making excuses for Hen
Did Lettie ever drop one word of criticism.
He had been left to her care by an overindulgent mother
Who had spoiled him from the day he was born.
Probably many of the neighbors
Felt that this final act was the most worthwhile thing

Hen had ever undertaken.
All of the neighbors had been in to see Lettie
And many had been interested in a glimpse at Hen.
Curious crowds had stood around looking at the house,
And the attendance at the funeral
Would have honored the most influential citizen.
Luella Pease had not been over to visit with Lettie
Although she had left some baked beans at the back door.
After the excitement had somewhat died down
Luella told her mother she was going over to see Lettie.
Her mother, knowing her happy faculty
For putting her foot in it,
Warned her to be careful about what she said,
And by no means to mention anything that would in any way
Bring Hen's manner of taking-off to mind.
Luella seemed shocked that her mother should mention such a thing.
Arriving at the house Luella started with the weather.
She said she was always glad to have it pleasant on Monday.
"I always say to Ma I'm glad if it's pleasant on Monday
On account of if it rains all the washings that don't dry."
Lettie agreed and remarked that Luella and her mother
Had a nice porch to use in case it rained.
"Yes" Luella said, "that's a fact, and your porch is too narrow."
Thinking that might seem critical, she hastened to add:
"But of course you've got a nice attic
To hang things in."

Women vs. Horses

Jake Penderson never appeared on the road
Behind anything but an extra good piece of horseflesh.
He seemed to have superior judgement in his choosing;
Either that or there was some magic in his touch
Which made even ornery beasts give in to him.
He had been known to hitch a confirmed kicker to his buggy
And drive it up and down the street in perfect comfort.
When he'd approach a cantankerous horse
It would usually put its ears back and roll its eyes.
Often it would tremble and break out into a sweat.

But Jake would rub its neck and talk to it
And get complete control in no time.
When it came to selecting and getting on with women
Jake had three times proved a failure.
He lived longest with the first one
But after five years of steady argument
He left her and she got a divorce.
His second venture lasted about the same length of time.
Then after a long wait, in his middle age, he tried again.
There was a separation within a year.
Miss Petty met Jake the day after the papers
Had announced that he had been granted a divorce.
He'd just tied his sleek chestnut mare to the hitching bar
And stepped out of his shining buggy.
"Jake Penderson" Miss Petty said, "I can't never make out
How come a man that's such an awful good handler o' hosses
Can make such a fool mess o' things with women."
Jake ran his hand over the chestnut mare's neck.
"Well Miss Petty, it's this way:
Give me the right bit and there isn't a horse I can't handle."
He scuffed up a pile of dirt with his shoe.
"But so far I've never heard of any invention
That has a mite of effect on a woman's mouth."

Christmas 1945

It was all just as he remembered it:
The long village street with the irregular Green
About half-way down.
There were wreaths in windows and on doors,
And colored lights that would come to life at night.
Yes, and there was the big tree on the edge of the Green.
He was glad they had all these things back,
Just as they used to be before he had gone away.
He thought, as he drove along slowly,
Of all the strange places where he'd remembered that street.
The thought of it had often been the thing
That kept him going ahead—
Remembering to make himself forget.

64

He found so many packages
In the post office at Brayley's store,
That he had to make two trips to the pickup truck.
When he came back for the second lot
Old man Peters, who was sitting back of the stove,
Stuck his head out and said:
"Well Charlie, looks as though you'd bought out
A hul city store on your way back from discharge camp."
Charlie, who had almost forgotten the life of four years back,
Suddenly felt the home warmth in the old man's bantering tone.
After he had gone out, old man Peters shook his head.
"Can't see how they stood what they did.
I recollect, musta been 'bout a year ago now,
Charlie's father had a letter tellin' as how
The boy's outfit had got caught there in It'ly,
Been under shell fire fer a week, day and night.
Course Charlie spoke of dodgin' high explosives,
Makin' light of it.
I recollect he spoke of spendin' th' night
In a barn with the front blowed away."
Brayley sat with a far away look in his eyes.
Then he said:
"I recollect that letter.
I know it come just this time o' year.
The boy said he slep' in a manger."

Aunt Betsy

That small unpainted house almost hidden by bushes
Had been Aunt Betsy's home since childhood.
In the early days the yard had been kept up
But when all the work about the place
Had to be done by Aunt Betsy herself,
The front yard gradually went its own way.
Aunt Betsy never used the front door
And everybody got used to following the path to the back.
There they'd find her on pleasant days
Busy in her garden or with her chickens.
She'd invite them to sit down on her back porch

And she'd bring out some of her homemade wine—
Elderberry, currant or dandelion.
She was never too busy to stop for a visit.
She didn't mind a little gossip now and then
But she never let her love of spice
Over-flavor anything she passed around.
During the best of the year she went to the village,
Usually getting a lift from someone passing.
She always carried a basket on her arm.
She might have eggs in it for the store
Or she might have a mess of peas to leave at someone's door.
Often she carried a bunch of flowers for someone who was sick.
Many people said a call from Aunt Betsy when you were sick
Was as good as a dose of tonic.
One day she was on her way home from the village
When a car stopped and a man asked her to ride.
She'd never seen him or the woman beside him
But she never hesitated when a ride was offered.
She leaned forward sitting on the edge of the back seat.
As usual she set out to find who these people were.
They seemed to know who she was and where she lived.
Then it came to her who they might be.
"You ain't the new principal up to the Academy by any chance?"
The car was slowing up in front of her house.
"Yes, that's right" he said, "and this is my wife."
As the car stopped Aunt Betsy shook hands with them.
"Thanks very much for the ride and meetin' you—well—
"I've been havin' a better time than I thought I was."

Heavenly Bookkeeping

Gideon Small had passed through youth
Without straying from the path of rectitude.
He often referred to his early days
When he was speaking of the sins of modern youth.
His farm was as well run as any in the valley.
His herd of Jerseys was the best in the county.
His house was as neat and well-cared-for as his barns,

66

Which wasn't always the case among his neighbors.
The life of his family was likewise well-ordered.
Gideon looked upon his relations with his Maker
As he did those with his neighbors.
He did his duty by both as he saw it
And expected like justice to be meted out to him.
He and his family did their part, as he considered it,
By attending church regularly
And making generous contributions each year.
The fact that he was prospered
Confirmed him in his beliefs.
Then came a year when there was sickness in his family
And during the winter he lost three of his best Jerseys.
The next year an early frost hit his crops.
Gideon grew bitter.
His mouth was a straight line and he didn't smile.
That year's end, when the time for his annual church contribution
Came around, he handed his check to the treasurer.
"I figger" he said as he buttoned his coat,
"I've lived an upright and Christian life.
I've kep' the commandments and supported the church."
He leaned toward the treasurer and spoke slowly.
"I been figgerin' up what I lost by storm and pestilence—
Things the Bible says was always sent to punish.
I don't figger I deserve any such treatment.
Just as a matter o' common justice it ain't right."
He started toward the door.
"You'll see I cut my church donation right in half.
I've kep' my part of the bargain,
But I ain't been met half way."

On Taking Orders

When great-grandfather Skelton built his house,
Back on the hills at the foot of the mountain,
He wasn't troubled by the steep and winding road
That had to be traveled to get to it.
The land on the high flat was good and fairly level.

He cut the timber for his house on his own mountain land
And all his life he was beholden to nobody.
If the view from the hill, which included much of the valley,
Was considered when he placed his house
He never was known to mention it
Until he was old, when he talked of many things
About which he'd always been silent.
It did seem that the steady living with the steadfast hills
Entered into the warp and woof of his being.
By the time his grandson, Elisha, owned the farm
The blood had grown thin as had the soil.
Elisha had the family physique and the old independence
But the success of his forebears was never his.
When the need for cash got most pressing
He would cut some logs on the mountain land.
Then he'd sell stove wood down in the village.
One fall day a shining car climbed the hill
Toward the shabby Skelton farmhouse.
By the time the city surgeon who was driving,
Had been jolted by holes and narrowly escaped edging rocks,
He was not in a pleasant frame of mind.
He stopped by the kitchen door and blew his horn.
No sign of life appeared anywhere.
He pressed the horn button down and let it blow.
Just as he was about to start his motor the door opened.
Elisha stood holding the door.
"What yu want?" he shouted in a high voice.
The surgeon turned the switch and called out:
"I hear you've got some wood to sell."
Elisha came out and leaned against a porch post.
"Ain't got any cut up jest now" he said.
"Well good heavens, you can cut some can't you?"
Elisha had by then decided that no amount of money
Would make him have any dealings with a man like the surgeon.
"I don't want it until November anyhow" the surgeon went on.
"You can take orders can't you?"
Elisha straightened up and reached for the latch.
"No sir, I don't take orders from nobody," he shouted.
He opened the door and disappeared into the kitchen.

68

Too Hurried

Brownie had been a member of the Todd family
Three years before they had moved into the village.
Sidney had picked her out of his herd of cattle
As the one he'd save when he had the auction.
During the time they'd had her in the village
She had justified the wisdom of his choice.
Having her to milk twice a day and to drive to pasture
And having her calf to look after each year
Had kept Sidney from feeling the loss of the farm too much.
When Brownie died, he and his wife felt as though
They'd lost a member of the family.
At first Sidney thought he wouldn't get another cow.
There were just the two of them and it might be cheaper
To buy what little milk and butter they'd use.
But they missed the homemade butter and the cottage cheese
And also the small income Sidney got
From the milk and cream he sold his neighbors.
Most of all he missed the company of Brownie.
One day he heard Nathan Severance had a cow to sell
And he walked the three miles out to see her.
"I'll just drop down and look 'er over" he told his wife.
Nathan took him into the barn and he looked the cow over.
Then he led her out where the light was better.
She seemed all right and she looked some like Brownie.
He made up his mind right off but he didn't let Nathan know.
Nathan led her back into the barn
And then insisted that Sidney come in and sit.
They drew up before the kitchen stove and pulled out their pipes.
Sidney found himself talking about Brownie
As though there'd never be another cow like her.
Then he admitted this cow he'd just seen
Reminded him a lot of the lost favorite.
Nate suddenly let his chair down and took his pipe out.
"Hold on there Sidney! Hold on!
You're hurryin' things.
First you know we'll be doin' business."

Not a Joiner

The Ambersons had occupied the parsonage less than a year
When members of the congregation became critical.
They liked the Reverend Arthur Amberson very much
But the women found his wife aloof and uncooperative.
At first they decided she wasn't very well
But they found that was not the reason she stayed home.
She always seemed to be doing something for her husband.
Not that he really demanded all her time
But that she demanded that he take it.
She did attend the Ladies Aid meetings but took no part—
She even refused any office in the Missionary Society.
Reluctantly the women gradually came to the conclusion
That she was not adapted to being a minister's wife.
One of the deacon's daughters, who lived away,
Came home for her vacation just about this time
And she learned of the dissatisfaction among the women.
Nobody had ventured to speak to Mrs. Amberson
But the deacon's daughter agreed to see what she could do.
She found Mrs. Amberson so pleasant she almost gave up her mission.
A Grange fair was coming shortly and she asked Mrs. Amberson
If she, like everybody else, was busy in preparation.
"No" Mrs. Amberson said. "I'm not a member of the Grange."
The way she shut her mouth encouraged her caller
To proceed with the execution of her mission.
"I suppose your work in the Mission Society
And other church groups does take most of your time" she said.
Finding she did little there by her own confession
She asked her if she happened to be an Eastern Star.
She also mentioned the Rebekahs and the P.T.A.
The answer came to be a simple "No" and tight-shut lips.
Finally Mrs. Amberson relaxed and sat back in her chair.
She rocked a minute and then smiled as she said:
"No, I really don't belong to any of these organizations.
As a matter of fact, I just belong to Arthur."

Arrival

Steve Henderson sat in the sun
On the steps of the general store.
The sign on the store, furnished by the firm
Whose goods were advertised at either end,
Informed the public that this was HAVEN'S GENERAL STORE.
Steve had both hands resting on his cane
And he seemed completely absorbed
In something on the ground at his feet.
However his bushy eyebrows hid roving eyes.
Without raising his head he'd follow
Anything that moved along the road.
When he had to change his position to see,
His head and shoulders moved together
As though he had a chronic stiff neck.
Now and then somebody would stop with a foot on the lower step
And pass the time of day with Steve.
Steve did most of the listening.
If he spoke he first let fly from his mouth
And shifted his cud of fine-cut.
He was sitting alone one morning
When a car came around the corner and stopped.
The driver got out and approached Steve who didn't seem to see him.
To his "Good morning" Steve moved his shoulders
And fired to the left.
"Can you tell me how to get to Stockbridge Corners?"
Firing again to the left Steve said "Nope."
"You mean you can't tell me how to get to Stockbridge Corners?"
Again Steve chewed rapidly and fired and said "Nope."
The stranger got right in front of Steve.
"Would you mind telling me why you can't give this information?"
Steve humped his shoulders and twisted his face
Into his nearest approach to a smile.
Firing again and then chewing rapidly he said:
"B'gol you're there."

Inseparable Companions

John drove the wagonette up from the depot
And stopped with a loud "Whoa" in front of the store.
He climbed down from his seat and went in to look at the slate.
The slate hung behind the front door
And when anybody wanted to take a train
He wrote his order for John to call for him on it.
"Call at Ellery Slade's for three passengers, down train."
John looked at the orders for the next train,
Pulled out his pipe and joined the sitters for a few minutes.
Somebody asked John if it was true
That the Baileys had left that morning on the up train.
John admitted as much and opined that they'd never come back.
"From all they said I guess they was glad to get out."
Someone wondered where they'd lived before,
And recalled they'd only been in town a few years.
Patching information together it appeared
That the Baileys had been frequent movers.
Everybody said they'd seemed to fit right in at first.
They'd rented a house and spoke of buying if they liked it.
They were high in praise of the town,
But someone recalled, they usually damned the one they'd moved from.
They'd gone in for everything like church and Grange.
Then after the first year they began to grow less active.
Finally Mrs. Bailey, who was out-and-out critical,
Had even joined a club in the next town.
It was said she didn't hesitate to tell the members
All the unpleasant things she could about the village.
John looked at the clock and emptied his pipe.
"Well, from what they said, this new place they're headed for
Is about as near th' Gardin of Eden
As they're likely to find in this vale of tears."
"That Mis' Bailey, she'll find th' sarpint there fore long."
The storekeeper leaned on the counter.
"Yep. They won't be a mite better off there.
Whole trouble is that wherever that woman goes
She has t' take Mis' Bailey along with 'er."

72

O Sweet Content

The Professor and his wife had stayed
Much later than they ever had since they bought the place.
For the first time there were no waiting classes
For the Professor to get back to.
The long awaited retirement
Which he'd looked forward to and dreaded had come.
The week before the opening of the University
He had found himself in the hurried state of mind
That those days had brought on for nearly a half-century.
Then he gradually realized he didn't have to go to anything.
Today life still seemed good to him as he turned from the fire
To his favorite view down the valley.
The cold gray clouds portended snow
And the warmth of the fire was cheering.
He almost wished they hadn't planned to go South,
Even though that had long been a cherished part
Of the retirement years' plan.
He tried to imagine how it would look
When snow covered the valley.
He recalled his boyhood days on hills not so far away.
John Burke came in with an armful of wood,
Maple, fresh cut and smelling of sap.
The Professor spoke of that smell
Which reminded him of maple sugar time.
"Do you find yourself sort of dreading the winter, John?"
John leaned over the hearth and shook the snow and sawdust
From his sheep-lined coat.
"Wal, Perfessor, it's this way with me."
He took off his cap and leaned against the mantel.
"Come late November, settin' by th' kitchin stove,
I sez t' myself, I sez:
"M' shed's full o' wood and th' barn's full o' hay;
We got a barr'l o' flour in th' butt'ry
And a crock er more o' pork and some fair cider down cellar.
And settin' there b' the kitchin stove
I hitches up m' heavy wool socks
And I sez t' m' self, I sez,
'LET 'ER SNOW b' Judast, LET 'ER SNOW!'."

Rainy Days

The guests at Fisk's Farm Boarding House
Had been herded together in the big double parlor
By so many rainy days that their nerves were frayed.
For over a week it had rained for at least part of each day
And for two solid days it had just poured.
The card players had almost come to blows
And Miss Emmet, who was always cold,
Had finally bundled up as for winter and camped out on the porch.
Professor Ketchum had tried to spread a little cheer
By suggesting that each one sit down and decide
Whether to give up, sit down and mildew to death,
Or to grow webbed feet and feathers and enjoy the new life.
Two recent additions to the list of guests
Furnished some interest to the old timers
Who had come each year since Mrs. Fisk opened her doors.
One of the newcomers donned wet-weather clothing
And sloshed through meadows and along muddy roads
And came in exuding love of nature, especially in liquid form.
The shut-ins first warned her against colds and pneumonia.
After a while they hoped she'd encounter something fatal.
The other new arrival took the state of the weather
As something directed at him personally.
He spoke as though the Fisks were getting his money
Under false pretenses.
He noted many other places where it had been sunny.
The sun had shone for days on end in New Hampshire.
Finally he encountered Mr. Fisk as he passed the porch
Where he was trying to stare the dripping landscape
Out of countenance.
"I'd like to ask you" the bored boarder said,
"Whether it really rains here all of the time?"
Mr. Fisk limbered up his chew
And added his mite to the general dampness.
"No, I wouldn't say that" he said speaking deliberately.
"Sometimes it snows."

A Matrimonial Fee

Sylvester Harmon, bachelor,
Had lived alone on his farm for some years.
He had always been handy around the house
So, when his mother died, he could get along.
He was very saving and his board bill
Was never anything to worry about.
He raised practically all he ate,
Being particular not to eat what he had to buy.
One October day the village was amazed
To see Sylvester, on a week day, dressed in his Sunday clothes.
He stopped his ancient Ford in front of the store
And went in to get his biweekly newspaper.
His car was washed and looked almost polished.
He drove off up the valley leaving the sitters
Speculating as to what might be happening.
He stopped at Mis' Stephen's boarding house
And at once the widow Bucklin came out in her Sunday best.
She got in and Sylvester drove to the next village.
They both got out at the Methodist parsonage.
In a short time they came out and she got into the car.
Sylvester took a large basket of winter squash out of the back
And took them to the Minister who was on the porch
Waiting to see the newlyweds off.
"There's yer fee, Parson, and they're awful good squashes."
Sylvester and his bride drove over the mountain
Where he surprised a niece with news of his marriage
And the fact that they were spending a week's honeymoon there.
Three weeks later the Methodist parson answered a rap at the door.
There stood Sylvester with another large basket of squash.
"Why Mr. Harmon," the minister said looking at the squashes,
"You have already generously supplied me with squash—
In fact with more than we can reasonably make way with."
"Yep" Sylvester said in his clipped way of speaking.
"I know I give you one lot, but yu see, Parson,
I got so much better bargain than I ever expected,
You just gotta take this lot too."

A Generous Target

Lawyer Sears was a born gambler.
Taking a chance was his chief delight.
When he began his practice he was always taking chances,
Usually long ones, on many of his clients.
As his practice increased he grew more conservative
As far as his professional services went.
Otherwise he was forever buying real estate
Or almost anything where there was a gamble involved.
His poker game was that of an expert
And he rarely missed a week without at least one evening
Devoted to serious poker playing.
Mrs. Sears was much opposed to any card playing
And when, after they had been married a short time,
She found that her husband not only played cards,
Which she had known, but that he played for money
She was so upset that he gave up cards entirely for some years.
Gradually he got back into his old habits
When he was attending court in other places
And in due time his wife accepted his sinning
Though in no way condoning it.
All of Lawyer Sears' churchgoing religion
Was in his wife's name,
And she was faithful enough to cover two souls' salvation.
She often brought visiting clergymen home to meals
Hoping, perhaps, to stir some churchly interest in her husband.
One Sunday, a supply minister during the regular one's vacation
Had, in the course of his sermon,
Made some scorching remarks about the growing habit of gambling.
Knowing he was to dine at the Sears', one of the congregation,
A former friend of the clergyman,
Warned him of Lawyer Sears' gambling propensities.
The young minister, deciding to clear the air at once,
As soon as he had said grace turned to Lawyer Sears,
"Mr. Sears, while retracting nothing of what I said,
I trust if you hear of some remarks I made this morning
You will not feel that there was anything personal meant.
You see I, er———."
Lawyer Sears held the carving knife and fork

Poised over the Sunday roast.
"Don't worry a mite, young man" he said.
"It would be an uncommonly weak sermon
That didn't hit me somewhere."

The Latest Decision

The usual after-dinner struggle to keep awake
Was obviously going on in the court room.
One of the side judges was shielding his closed eyes
By resting his head on his spread out hand.
The presiding judge leaned forward in his chair,
Either straining to hear, or to keep awake, or both.
From the open window came the sawing of a locust
And now and then the clatter of a passing wagon.
The officers of the court, the sheriff and constables,
Had tipped their chairs back against the wall
And were sleeping peacefully.
Most of the jurors were paying attention to the witness
Except for one old man in the back row
Who kept drifting off and then coming to with a start.
Then he'd look around to see if anyone noticed.
The defending lawyer was a nattily dressed New Yorker.
There was nothing sleepy about him
As he fired questions at the rather slow-witted witness.
The local prosecuting attorney sat slouched in his chair
With his long legs stretched out in front of him.
The visiting attorney snapped out a question.
Very deliberately the local lawyer said;
"I object to that question, Your Honor."
The Judge looked through his bushy eyebrows and barked:
"Objection sustained."
The New York attorney faced the court.
In a rather patronizing tone he informed the court
That a very recent decision had been handed down
Which would make the evidence in question admissible.
Looking around at the jury and audience he added, smiling,
"Probably news of this most recent decision
Has not as yet penetrated to these remote parts."

The Judge leaned over toward the attorney.
"This court just handed down a decision to the effect
That this evidence is not admissible.
If the learned gentleman from New York
Knows of any more recent decision than that,
This court will be glad to hear about it."

A Jawer

There was no real reason for hurry
But Lemira Hoddle was rushing around in her house
As though the day of judgement was at hand.
It was one of those waiting days of autumn
When the warm drowsiness of the air
Invited the soul.
In the yard in front of the Hoddle place
There was a gay colored carpet of leaves from the maples.
A belated cricket fiddled from the marble doorstep
But Mrs. Hoddle never paid any heed.
She was getting her house ready for winter
Although there had been only a few frosty nights.
She had argued and stewed until in desperation
Alfred had set the stove up in the sitting room,
Where she was now busy blacking the already shining pipe.
Alfred had wheeled the stove up to the front porch
And with rollers and a plank he'd rolled it through the hall.
Lemira had accompanied him every step
Admonishing him about the paint on one side
Or to be careful when he went through the door
Not to rub his dirty clothes on the wall paper.
It was with pleasure that Alfred noticed
That the stove had shed a small pile of ashes on the carpet.
When Lemira stepped in them and tracked on through the parlor
As she rushed around that way to get in front of the stove,
He chuckled with delight in spite of what might come later.
He'd got the stove placed on the zinc
And was escaping through the hall when Lemira rushed after him.
"My lands!" she said brushing her hair from her face,
"I do believe you're gettin' so deef

You don't hear more 'n half I say to you."
Alfred went on down the steps
And picked up the wheelbarrow handles.
"Well if I don't hear more 'n quarter
I've heered enough" he said, not looking up.

A Heedless Horse

Through most of the twenty years Hiram Eddy had been a bookkeeper
He had dreamed that some day he'd own a farm.
He took several farming magazines
And read every book in the library on farm life.
His long-suffering wife was annually dragged to the country
Where Hiram looked over likely farms
He'd read about in the numerous agents' lists,
Which he kept in a drawer in his desk.
Finally he was told by his doctor, after a bout with influenza,
That he should really do something out in the air.
The result was that in the spring Henry and his wife
Moved onto a forty acre farm at the edge of the village.
They'd lived there a year and Henry's health was better.
He'd already enjoyed the company of a pig
And the kitchen was filled with peeping chickens
Temporarily hospitalized near the stove.
Finally he decided he must have a horse.
He studied up about horses and talked to several men.
He decided he really knew something about horses at last
And he went across the valley to look at one offered for sale.
She looked good and sleek in the stall
And Hiram suggested the owner let her loose
So she could limber up around the barnyard.
Rather reluctantly the farmer slipped the halter off
Saying that she was used to being led out to water.
The mare started out and ran into the side of the door.
"She's new here" he said giving her a shove.
She grazed a lumber wagon and bumped into a tree.
Hiram looked at the farmer. "Blind, isn't she?"
The farmer laughed. "Blind? That mare blind?
Hell no, she ain't blind.
She just doesn't give a damn."

Beyond The Pale

Since Miss Scovill had taken boarders for years
Having a new one wasn't in itself so unusual.
The difference was that the new one planned to stay a long time.
All of her other boarders were clerks in the store or mill
Or school teachers, who usually married or moved from town.
Mr. Anthony, the new boarder, just got off the train
And came to Miss Scovill's, directed by the station agent.
He took his room for a week, and then told his landlady
That he'd like to send for a few of his own pieces of furniture
And take his room and the adjoining one for a year.
He didn't seem to have any job in town and at first
Miss Scovill had been suspicious.
Then she found he belonged to an old New England family
And that his father had been a clergyman.
He also confided that he "did a little painting."
In due time it seemed evident
That his painting did not support him.
He was full of interest in the village people
And Miss Scovill was glad to give him
Her version of the family history of each one.
Twice he had tried to describe to her
A man he'd seen several times.
What had struck him was the fact that nobody spoke to him.
At least they all were very reserved with him.
Finally, one day as Miss Scovill was sweeping her walk,
Mr. Anthony hurried through the gate.
"There's the man I've been describing to you—
The one everybody seems so cold toward."
Miss Scovill peered at the man and then sniffed.
"He seems perfectly normal. Why is he treated this way?"
Miss Scovill first answered with several swift strokes
With her broom.
Then she said as if mentioning a criminal:
"He's spendin' his principal."

An Isolationist

Oliver Humper's farm was on a side road
On a hill to the east of the village.
The upper meadow ended in a stone wall
Which separated it from a rocky pasture.
This was gradually ended by the ever-encroaching woods.
Oliver and his wife were the only remnants
Of a family which had once filled the farmhouse.
They had finally taken care of the old folks
And then been left there, childless, to keep the place going.
After his parents died Oliver bought some acres
Up on the mountain adjoining his own land.
He bought it cheap and folks thought he was wise.
Next he bought some land on the other side
That adjoined his pasture to the south.
Then he bought a rock-ribbed piece, north,
With nothing much on it but scrub pine.
There would never be any good timber on it,
Not in Oliver's time at any rate.
Then the opinion makers around the store stove
Began to wonder what had come over Oliver.
He'd kept right on buying, first on one side and then on another.
One day when they heard his back line had moved again
By the acquisition of more mountain land,
Oliver dropped into the store.
Old man Stevens decided he'd find out
Whether Oliver was plain crazy, as he suspected, or not.
So he asked Oliver what he thought he was doing
Buying up all of outdoors this way.
Oliver looked over his glasses and said:
"Don't like t' have folks ownin' land next t' mine.
That's why."

Head vs. Heart

Except for one or two, the women in the valley
Had never taken much part in politics.
One spinster had declared that if there was one thing
The men could do without calling on the women to help

For the lands sake, let them do it.
A few young women who had been interested in city politics
Came to live in the village and they organized a "study group."
One fall soon after, there was unusual excitement over election.
Usually strongly Republican, there had grown up
A group which showed an interest in the Democratic party
Much to the disgust of some of the elders.
Mary Hickson was one of these.
She hadn't lived in the valley long.
She set out on a regular vote-getting campaign for the Democrats.
She went up to see Sidney Rawson.
She didn't know he'd been prominent and active
In the Republican party in the state for years.
She'd only known him since ill health
Had confined him to the house most of the time.
He was glad to see her; his mind was alert and he liked young folks.
He led her into arguments in support of the Democratic candidate.
Finally she arose, feeling she had a convert.
She shook Sidney's hand with enthusiasm as she said:
"I'll be expecting you to vote for my candidate
When you go down to the village a week from Tuesday."
Sidney looked at her with a fatherly smile.
"Well, Miss, I've certainly enjoyed your visit.
You've made out as good a case as could be made for your party.
But, sorry as I am to disappoint you, I'm still voting Republican."
He hobbled over to open the door.
"You see, Miss, my trouble ain't with my head,
It's m' heart."

A Raw Deal

Mrs. Newcomer found Henry sitting under a tree
In the midst of the half-mowed lawn.
He started to get up and then saw he was too late.
He settled back against the tree looking hopelessly disconsolate.
A few concerned questions brought forth his sad story.
It was the outrageous conduct of his housekeeper
Who had been in his home since the passing of his wife
Some two months before.

He wound up his story with some show of fire:
"She's give me a raw deal and I ain't goin' t' stan' it."
The facts were that Henry's wife had waited on him
Hand and foot while he did a lot of heavy loafing.
He might go so far as to get some polewood cut
And drawn into the yard. He might work up a little of it
But many a time the neighbors saw his wife out chopping wood
While Henry was telling how the world should be run, down at
    Brayley's.
He was supposed to have weak lungs
So he couldn't do much work especially in cold air.
His housekeeper was a mild-appearing woman
And after the first few weeks Henry began to leave things
Much as he'd done with his wife.
Henry told Mrs. Newcomer she hadn't complained a bit.
He had got considerable wood bucked up
And she fetched that in and never said a word.
This morning she'd told him there wasn't any wood
And he'd told her she might cut some of the pole wood
That was still in the yard and he showed her where the axe was.
"Today noon I goes home, hot and wore out" he said.
He'd sat down at the kitchen table right off.
"Dishes was set out as usual and I thinks t' m'self:
'Guess she took th' hint 'bout that wood.' "
Henry flipped his battered hat at a visiting fly.
"So I seddown and histed the cover off'n a dish
And jabbed m' fork into a pertater.
Mis' Newcomer, the pertaters was raw."
Henry in his anger got to his feet.
"And th' beets in another dish was raw,
And jest then she set a platter o' meat down,
And by judast, that was raw."
Henry paused for breath.
"What madded most was her setting down by the winder
And sayin' in that meek meechin way o' hern:
'Yu see, I told you I was out o' wood this mornin'.' "

On a Covered Bridge

Henry Stiles had told Joe, his hired man,
To take the load of hay on the rack
To the barn on the upper farm across the river.
Then he'd driven to the village to do some trading.
Joe had hitched up the team after the noon chores
And started down the road with the load of hay.
One of the Waller boys happened to be near the road
Fixing the fence in front of his house.
Joe stopped to talk as he usually did.
The other Waller brother came up out of the hatchway
Wiping his mouth with the back of his hand.
Shortly Joe slipped down off the load of hay.
A little later he came up out of the hatchway
Wiping his mouth with the back of his hand.
He'd had three tumblers of an innocent tasting drink
The Waller brothers had been making
By adding a few things to the cider the fall before.
They'd just been testing the well-worked result.
By the time Joe again got under way with his load
He was carrying a considerable one himself.
A little later Henry Stiles, returning from the village
Came on his hired man blocking the entrance
To the long covered bridge with his load of hay.
As Henry stopped, Joe emerged from the bridge
Crowding past the load.
"No sir," he said waving toward the load
"I mebbe could get in that end o' the bridge.
But by judast, when I see how she narrows down this end,
I knowed the load wouldn't go through, not never."

Scenery

The westward moving sun
Had already filled the valley with shadows.
The long line of autumn-tinted mountains to the east
Looked like a tapestry hanging loosely from the sky.
The whole landscape seemed set like a painting.

84

Only at the edge of the dark line of shadow
Did the trees and bushes seem real and alive.
There the colors stood out against the spruces.
A man with a pack on his back and a stick in his hand
Came up the road walking sidewise to get the view.
He put his pack down beside the road
And slowly removed his hat
As his eyes followed the line of mountains.
Finally he'd had his fill and he turned to his pack.
Just then he discovered a man with his arms on the fence
Looking away toward the sunlit mountains
Above the creeping shadow.
Pleased to have someone to share it with the traveler said:
"It's a magnificent view you have here."
The old man's eyes turned for a minute to the speaker
And then back to the view.
Faint puffs of smoke arose from his pipe.
Speaking a little louder the stranger said again:
"I say you have a fine view here."
Again the eyes moved and faint puffs of smoke arose.
Getting close to the old man the stranger shouted:
"Nice view you've got here!"
Slowly the old man turned and removed his pipe.
Then he spoke very quietly;
"Well, what do you want t' do,
Argue about it?"

Final Escape

The Binney family had long been a problem.
They lived in what had once been a fine old farmhouse
Just across the line in New York.
The old folks, gaunt and toothless,
Had managed to live there paying rent to absent owners
Only when eviction seemed absolutely certain.
There were always visiting babies present
As well as children of varying ages and assorted parents.
As a general rule the father was "away working."
One of the neighbors had complained

That there was too much new fangled "mixed hygiene" there
And that something ought to be done about it.
As a result the new rector from the village dropped in.
Father Binney was most cordial and sat the clergyman down
In the overstuffed chair on the porch.
Several daughters and in-laws peeked out of the windows
Or rushed out to seize grubby children.
Ma Binney came out with a batch of peas she was shelling.
Chickens wandered up the broken steps
And several lanky hounds snooped around the yard.
A few nights later the rector stopped around again.
A thunderstorm was in the making and there was an eerie light
Which brought the colors out and hid some of the drabness.
As the rector approached the house a dog under the step growled.
Before the rector's hair had resumed normal position
He was further startled by the sound of a voice.
It was coming from the house and shouting threats
Of hellfire and damnation to all who did not repent
And prepare for the imminent end of the world.
The shouting was punctuated by crashes of static.
A flash of lightning showed the Binney family,
Some sitting on chairs, some on boxes and some on the floor.
They were listening to the only station they could get.
Suddenly there was a vivid flash of lightning, a crackling sound,
And then a crash of thunder which rattled the windows.
The dim light of the radio went out leaving dense darkness
And a silence that could be cut with a knife.
Somebody moved a chair near the door where the rector stood.
Then from the darkness came the deep voice of Father Binney.
"I don't give much of a damn if the end of the world does come.
I got kin folks over in V'mont
And I'll just go over there and stay."

What's Hers is Her Own

Dwight Hutton and his wife were both strong-minded.
In spite of that they had lived together for thirty years
And they were still in love.
Probably the reason they got along

86

Was that each allowed the other to live his own life.
Dwight attended to his law practice as he saw fit
And his wife never thought of making any suggestions.
In the household she ruled supreme—at least Dwight said she should.
Now and then he did make remarks about something he didn't like
But little heed was paid to complaints or suggestions.
One time he did express an adverse opinion
And he expressed it in no uncertain terms.
It was the time his wife decided to get an oil stove,
To replace the perfectly good wood-burning one in the kitchen.
Dwight had mentioned every bad thing he could think of
In opposition to the new-fangled kerosene burners.
When he got all through, his wife told him
She had bought one anyhow.
He looked at her for a minute and then said:
"Well it's your house and your responsibility.
I've said my say and, if the damned thing blows up
And burns the house down, you can't say you weren't warned."
He picked up his hat, hesitated, went over and kissed her
And went out the door.
They had been using the oil range a month or more.
Dwight was sitting on the front porch waiting for supper.
He heard rapid steps out in the kitchen and his wife's voice.
"Dwight, something's wrong with this stove.
It's blazing up and I can't regulate it."
Dwight didn't even turn his head.
"Phone for the fire department. They'll fix your stove" he called.
He heard her call, shouting into the phone.
A wisp of smoke came sifting through the hall.
He heard the fire engine roaring up the street.
It stopped in front of the house and the men rushed up the drive.
"Where's the fire? The call came from here?" the chief shouted.
Dwight still sat with his chair tilted against the house.
"I don't know a thing about it" he said very calmly.
"You better go and ask my wife back there in the kitchen.
It's her fire."

Population Center

Oh a hill the white tapering spire
Rose above the green leaves of the maples.
The faded red brick church with its white pillars
Was almost hidden by the big trees.
Two grass-grown tracks curved up from the road.
They led to the worn marble steps.
The sun shining through the leaves
Made shifting shadows on the fluted columns.
The columns made still, slanting shadows on the flagstones.
The grass-grown tracks led back of the church
To a stone wall covered with vines.
There was an iron gate
And beyond rows of stones, gray and moss-spotted,
And glistening monuments set in hedged plots.
An old man in checked gingham overalls and jumper
Was straightening one of the moss-spotted stones
Which stood near the gate.
A stranger came into the burying ground.
He had his coat under his arm and his straw hat in his hand.
"Say, are you acquainted around here?" he asked the old man.
"Lived here all m' life—so fur"
The old man said, straightening up a joint at a time.
The stranger didn't smile.
"Well I've been walking dusty roads in this burg
'Til I'm about worn out.
What I want to find is the thickly-settled part, if there is any."
The old man made a sweeping gesture toward the graveyard.
"Well sir" he said, "You're right plumb in the midst of it
Here and now."

Wedding Anniversary

Life at the Strong farm had not been easy.
Henry had inherited a mortgage
And worn-out land and run-down buildings.
He had married Eliza when she was just twenty
And together they had brought the farm back.

88

They had raised the money for the mortgage and a family besides.
Their fiftieth wedding anniversary had been about the first party
They'd ever felt they had time to join in.
They would never have thought of celebrating
But one of the daughters who lived nearby
Had the whole thing arranged before they heard.
They accepted the plans with some grumblings at first.
Then Eliza got into the spirit of it
And by the time the day had arrived
Henry had been helped into a boiled shirt
Without doing anything worse than a little quiet cursing.
They enjoyed the party so much that from then on
They began to go to things whenever they had a chance.
One evening they amazed everybody
By appearing at a Grange dance.
When Henry escorted Eliza to the floor
To make up a quadrille, the crowd broke into spontaneous applause.
Before they realized it they were having a party
Marking their sixtieth anniversary.
It was mostly an exhibition of grandchildren.
Toward the end of the day Henry was on the porch
Talking with three of his sons-in-law.
He was glad to sit quietly in a chair
But his wife was insisting on helping with the clearing up.
One of the sons-in-law asked Henry how he figured
That he had kept well to such a good old age.
Henry patted the arms of his chair.
"Well, when your mother-in-law and I got married
We made a little covenant like between us.
We agreed that when I got mad I'd keep my mouth shut.
When she got mad I'd go outdoors."
He stopped and whistled a few notes softly.
"I guess the outdoor life agreed with me."

Autumn Comes

The last time he'd seen the valley
The new leaves were just grown large enough
To catch the breeze and make moving shadows
On the fresh green grass.
The fields which sloped up toward the white farmhouse
Were plowed and sowed and smooth and waiting.
Every bush and twig and living thing
Had been stirring with life's renewal.
But today autumn had come to the valley.
The wooded hills showed reds and yellows
And the mountains were covered with a many-colored tapestry:
A curtain let down for the change of scene.
Crickets fiddled and at midday the locusts
Still trilled their summer song.
The meadows were a ripened, richer green
Where cattle leisurely cropped the grass
Or lay in the shade chewing a meditative cud.
Higher up the pastures were tanned by the summer's sun:
Brown squares cut off from the green meadows
By hedgerows of bronze and purple.
Up on the slope the farmhouse stood,
And nearby the red barn bulging with the gathered harvest.
Except for the cattle and the birds in the shocked corn,
No living thing intruded motion on the static scene.
It was set, as a painting, in the blending haze of autumn.
He felt he was an intruder;
That he should draw up beside the road
And take his place, a part of the peaceful picture.
Not to be something striving for a goal
But to be part of an ultimate arrival,
To share a few minutes of the patience of eternal time.
Slowly he withdrew,
Leaving the picture hanging there,
Feeling it would always stay, unchanged;
Knowing that only in his mind would it remain.